BARRON'S DOG BIBLES

Pomeranians

Karla S. Rugh, D.V.M., Ph.D.

Acknowledgments

Writing a book is never a solo effort, regardless of how many names appear on the title page. I especially thank Kristen Girardi, my editor at Barron's, for her expert guidance; my children, Christian and Aylecia, for their continued, if somewhat mysterious, faith in me; and my husband Jim, who makes it all possible.

About the Author

Karla S. Rugh, D.V.M., Ph.D., a graduate of Kansas State University, has been a veterinarian for more than 35 years. She completed a residency in veterinary anesthesiology at the University of Missouri-Columbia, where she also earned a Ph.D. in physiology. Dr. Rugh has written dozens of articles on various kinds of pets, including dogs, cats, rabbits, guinea pigs, and rats. She has also been a columnist for *Dog Fancy* magazine. Dr. Rugh is the author of *Miniature Schnauzers, A Complete Pet Owners Manual* published by Barron's Educational Series, Inc. This is her fourth book about dog care.

When she's not writing, Dr. Rugh enjoys spending time with her family, sewing, reading, working with her horses, and being a 4-H volunteer. She lives near Rocheport, Missouri with her family, which includes assorted furred and feathered members. Having enjoyed the companionship of many dogs since early childhood, she has given up trying to choose her favorite breed.

A Word About Pronouns

Many dog lovers feel that the pronoun "it" is not appropriate when referring to a pet that can be such a wonderful part of our lives. For this reason the Pomeranian in this book is referred to as "he" unless the topic specifically relates to female dogs. This by no means implies any preference, nor should it be taken as an indication that either sex is particularly problematic.

Cover Credits

Front cover and back cover: Shutterstock.

Photo Credits

Tara Darling: page 117; Cheryl A. Ertelt: pages 71, 81, 105, 120, 123, 124, 125; Shirley Fernandez/Paulette Johnson: pages 19, 20, 58, 79, 99, 119, 128, 138, 163; Isabelle Francais: page 130; Daniel Johnson: pages 44 (bottom), 45, 70, 100, 110, 132 (top and bottom), 133 (top and bottom), 134 (top and bottom), 135 (top and bottom), 136 (top and bottom), 137 (top and bottom); Paulette Johnson: pages vi, 4, 8, 11, 12, 18, 24, 33, 37, 38, 41, 42, 43, 47, 51, 52, 62, 65, 69, 76, 87, 93, 97, 106, 114, 141, 144, 147, 150, 152, 155, 159, 160, 170; Pets by Paulette: pages i, iii, v, 6, 7, 14, 21, 23, 26, 28, 30, 44 (top), 53, 55 (top and bottom), 72, 75, 98, 109, 142, 148, 164, 166; Shutterstock: page 38.

© Copyright 2010 by Barron's Educational Series, Inc.

All rights reserved.
No part of this publication may be reproduced or distributed in any form or by any means without the written permission of the copyright owner.

All inquiries should be addressed to:
Barron's Educational Series, Inc.
250 Wireless Boulevard
Hauppauge, New York 11788
www.barronseduc.com

ISBN-10: 0-7641-4365-4 (Book)
ISBN-13: 978-0-7641-4365-6 (Book)
ISBN-10: 0-7641-8678-7 (DVD)
ISBN-13: 978-0-7641-8678-3 (DVD)
ISBN-10: 0-7641-9687-1 (Package)
ISBN-13: 978-0-7641-9687-4 (Package)

Library of Congress Catalog Card No: 2009038686

Library of Congress Cataloging-in-Publication Data
Rugh, Karla S.
Pomeranians / Karla Rugh.
    p. cm. — (Barron's dog bibles)
ISBN-13: 978-0-7641-4365-6
ISBN-10: 0-7641-4365-4
ISBN-13: 978-0-7641-9687-4
ISBN-10: 0-7641-9687-1
    1. Pomeranian dog. I. Title.
SF429.P8R84 2009
636.76--dc22
                                                2009038686

Printed in China

9 8 7 6 5 4 3

CONTENTS

CONTENTS

A t first glance, it's easy to assume that the Pomeranian, with its tiny size and outrageously fluffy coat, doesn't do much other than sit around and look cute. That's not exactly true. Thanks to a working-dog ancestry, Pomeranians are intelligent, confident (even cocky), and active. They're cute, but they don't spend a lot of time sitting around. They're terrific companions, but only for people who understand and accept their unique characteristics.

If you're thinking about adopting a Pomeranian, it's important to learn everything you can about the breed before you take the big step into owner-ship. If you're already sharing your life with a Pom, you probably have more than a few questions about your furry friend. Either way, this book can help. It covers in detail all aspects of Pomeranian ownership, including the history of the breed; Pomeranian behavior (both good and bad); choosing a Pomeranian; puppy care and socialization; living with an adult Pomeranian; health care and nutrition; coat care and other grooming considerations; Pomeranian activities, competitions, and training; and taking care of a senior Pomeranian. Whether you already own a Pom or are just thinking about acquiring one, this book will give you a new appreciation for these lively, little dogs.

Chapter One

All About the Pomeranian

The Pomeranian is primarily a companion dog nowadays, but that tiny dynamo is a working dog at heart.

Pomeranian History

Today's Pomeranian is primarily a companion dog, but this wasn't always the case. Since much of how a dog acts is based on deep-seated ancestral traits, knowing your pal's origins and history can help you understand him. That, in turn, can lead to a stronger bond of friendship between you and your Pom.

From the Frozen North

The Pomeranian had its origins in northern Europe, rising from the Arctic or Spitz dogs of Iceland and Lapland. These working dogs were used for a variety of purposes, including pulling sleds, hunting, herding, and sounding alarms when danger threatened. They were well-suited to the work: hardy, athletic, devoted to their masters, and clothed in thick double coats that protected them from the frigid weather.

The Spitz dogs, which originally came in various sizes and colors, were popular in Germany as early as the sixteenth century. From this variety, five distinct types eventually emerged. The smallest of these was the *zwergspitz* or dwarf Spitz, which stood only 8½ to 11 inches (21–27.5 cm) at the shoulder. These little dogs came in many colors, including white, black, brown, wolf gray, and orange.

The *zwergspitz* became known as the Pomeranian not because it originated in Pomerania (a region of Germany and Poland on the southern coast of the Baltic Sea), but because breeders there bred the dogs down to a smaller size, though at 20 to 30 pounds (9–13.5 kg) they were still much larger than today's Poms. Interestingly, in Germany the breed is still called the Zwergspitz.

Broadening Horizons

The little *zwergspitz* started to gain popularity outside Pomerania when England's Queen Charlotte (the wife of George III) imported two white ones in 1767. The entire nation took notice of these royal dogs, whose status earned them a portrait by the renowned painter Thomas Gainsborough.

More than one hundred years later, in 1888, Queen Victoria, Queen Charlotte's granddaughter, succumbed to the charms of Marco, a 12-pound (5 kg) red sable Pomeranian she met in Italy. She brought him back to England, along with three females. Marco became Victoria's favorite companion, as well as a successful show dog. Gina, one of the imported females, was also a winner in the show ring. As a result of the queen's attention, Pomeranians skyrocketed in popularity in England, and toward the end of the ninteenth century, the smaller, red-coated dogs were clearly favored over the larger, white ones.

Breed Truths

All in the Family

The Pomeranian's closest relatives are the Norwegian Elkhound, the Schipperke, the German Spitz, the American Eskimo Dog, the Samoyed, and other members of the Spitz group of dogs.

The New World

By the time Victoria "discovered" Pomeranians, the breed had already made its way to the United States. In 1888, the first American Pomeranian was listed in the American Kennel Club stud book, and four years later the first Pom was shown in a dog show held in the United States. The breed achieved AKC recognition in 1900; the American Pomeranian Club was organized in that same year.

In the early twentieth century, the Pomeranian continued its rise in England and became one of the country's most popular breeds. It took a little longer for Poms to achieve this status in the United States, but in the 1930s they made their first appearance on the AKC's top 10 breeds list. In 1994, the breed again made the top 10 list, a status it retained for many years. To this day, the Pomeranian remains a popular breed not only in England and the United States, but around the world.

Famous Pomeranians: Then and Now

For more than four hundred years, Pomeranians have been popular with celebrities from all walks of life. They've sat on the laps or at the feet of all kinds of famous folks, from royalty to artists to movie stars. With that kind of popularity, it's no wonder that most of these fluffy little dogs think they're VIPs (Very Important Poms)!

Famous Pomeranians of the Past

Queen Charlotte and Queen Victoria weren't the only Pom fans in history. Here are some other famous Pom owners:

- Michelangelo, whose Pomeranian relaxed on a cushion while the artist painted the Sistine Chapel.
- Wolfgang Amadeus Mozart, who dedicated an aria to his Pom, Pimperl.
- Frederic Chopin, who didn't own a Pom, but was inspired by a lady friend's Pom to write *Valse des Petits Chiens* (Waltz of the Little Dog).
- Isaac Newton, whose Pom, Diamond, reportedly enjoyed chewing on the mathematician's papers.
- Martin Luther, who mentioned his Pomeranian, Belferlein, in his writings.
- Empress Josephine, Napoleon's wife, who supposedly owned several Poms, although some of these may have been Keeshonds.
- The Maharajah of Kapurthala, who had Pomeranians in the late ninteenth century.

Present-Day Celebrity Poms

The Pom's popularity with famous folks didn't stop in the 1800s. A number of modern-day celebrities have owned them too:

- Fran Drescher: Chester and Esther
- Hilary Duff: Macy, Bentley, and Griffin
- David Hasselhoff: Jenny and Killer
- Nicole Richie: Foxxy and Cleopatra
- LeAnn Rimes: Joey and Raven
- Britney Spears: Izzy
- Tammy Wynette: Killer
- Cindy Williams: Phoebe

Poms in Art

Through the years, Pomeranians have been frequent subjects of paintings, which isn't surprising given the breed's popularity. Reuben Cole painted Marco, Queen Victoria's Pom, in 1890, and Charles Burton Barger painted him in 1892. Listed below are some other artists and their Pom paintings:

- Francis Fairman (*Pomeranians*)
- Maud Earl (*Pomeranians with Apple, Pomeranians in the Park*)
- Wright Parker (*Roy*)
- Henry Crowther (*Pomeranian*)
- Thomas Gainsborough (*Pomeranian Bitch and Puppy, Perdita*)

Fun Facts

At the Movies

It's no surprise that Poms frequently appear on the big screen—their intelligence and athleticism undoubtedly make them easy to train for a variety of roles. And being cute doesn't hurt either! Look for Poms in the following flicks:

- *To Die For*
- *Harlem Nights*
- *Cadillac Man*
- *Enemy of the State*
- *Blade: Trinity*
- *Superman Returns*
- *Titanic*

The Pomeranian Breed Standard

The AKC Pomeranian breed standard is a blueprint for the perfect Pom, at least as far as breeders and judges are concerned. Few Poms meet every requirement of the standard, but top show dogs come as close as possible—that's why they're top show dogs.

Responsible breeders always consider both conformation (what the dog looks like) and temperament when selecting dogs for their breeding programs, but for a pet Pom, conformation isn't nearly as important as temperament. If your buddy is a gentle devoted friend, it doesn't really matter what he looks like. Conformation is important only if a fault could cause a health problem—for instance, if the teeth don't meet correctly, the dog might not be able to chew his food properly.

The standard starts off describing the general appearance of the Pom: "The Pomeranian is a compact, short-backed, active toy dog. He has a soft, dense undercoat with a profuse harsh-textured outer coat. His heavily plumed tail is set high and lies flat on his back. He is alert in character, exhibits intelligence in expression, is buoyant in deportment, and is inquisitive by nature." Farther down, the standard addresses temperament, describing the Pom as extroverted, intelligent, and vivacious.

The Pomeranian breed standard also goes into great detail describing the coat, with good reason: It's one of the breed's most distinctive features. The Pom's undercoat should be soft and dense, whereas the outercoat is long, straight, glistening, and harsh-textured. The coat is heavy ("abundant") on the neck, shoulders, and chest, forming a "frill," the mane of hair so typical of Poms. On the head and legs, the coat is shorter and denser than that on the body. The forequarters, thighs, and hind legs to the hocks are well-feathered. Long, harsh, spreading straight hair profusely covers the tail.

Even if your pal won't ever set paw in a show ring, it's still fun to find out what the experts consider to be the pinnacle of Pom-dom:

Breed Truths

Poms of Many Colors

All colors and patterns of Pomeranians are allowed and must be judged equally in conformation dog shows. Some of the colors often seen are red, orange, cream, sable, black, brown, and blue. Patterns include black and tan, brindle, and parti-color.

Size, Proportion, and Substance
- **Weight:** 3 to 7 pounds (1–3 kg) (4 to 6 pounds [2–3 kg] ideal for show dogs).
- **Frame:** Medium-boned, sturdy.
- **Proportions:** Distance from point of shoulder to point of buttocks is slightly shorter than height at withers. Distance from the brisket to the ground is half the height at the withers. Length of legs is in proportion to frame.

Head
- **Muzzle:** Rather short, straight, and fine.
- **Expression:** Alert, foxlike.
- **Skull:** Top is slightly rounded but not domed.
- **Ears:** Mounted high and carried erect.
- **Eyes:** Dark, bright, medium-sized, and almond-shaped.
- **Teeth:** Scissors bite (upper incisors overlap the lower incisors); one tooth out of alignment is acceptable.

Body
- **Neck:** Short, with base set well into shoulders to permit high head carriage.
- **Back:** Short, with level topline.
- **Body:** Compact, well-ribbed, with brisket extending to the elbow.
- **Shoulders and Front Legs:** Moderately muscled. Length of shoulder blade and upper arm are equal.
- **Forelegs:** Straight and parallel to each other; height from elbow to withers and from ground to elbow approximately equal.
- **Pasterns:** Straight and strong.

- **Feet:** Well-arched, compact, pointing straight ahead; dog stands well up on toes.
- **Hindquarters:** Hindquarter angulation balances that of forequarters. Buttocks are well behind the set of the tail. Thighs are moderately muscled.
- **Stifles:** Moderately bent; clearly defined.
- **Hocks:** Perpendicular to the ground.
- **Legs:** Straight and parallel to each other.
- **Tail:** Lies flat and straight on the back.

Move Out

The Pomeranian breed standard is quite specific in its description of how the ideal Pom should move. It clearly describes attributes that contribute to the breed's athleticism, as is fitting for a breed descended from hardworking Spitz dogs.

The gait should be smooth, free, balanced, and vigorous, with a good reach with the forequarters and a powerful drive with the hindquarters. The front and rear legs on each side move in line with each other, without being thrown inward or outward. The legs can converge slightly inward toward a center line to maintain balance. During movement, the topline should remain level, with the overall balance and outline maintained.

What's a Pomeranian Really Like?

Poms are cute little dogs, no doubt about it, but the "cuteness factor" is only part of the total Pom package. In fact, it's more like a bonus that comes with the other distinctive characteristics of the breed.

High Energy The Pomeranian is a toy breed, but there's nothing small about this little dog's energy level. Moving double-time is his idea of a normal pace. Your Pom won't be happy sitting around all day, so you'll need to make sure he gets plenty of exercise. He'll enjoy being in the yard, but he'll have more fun if you join him in some sort of active exercise every day.

COMPATIBILITY Is a Pomeranian the Best Breed for You?

ENERGY LEVEL	● ● ● ●
EXERCISE REQUIREMENTS	●
PLAYFULNESS	● ● ● ●
AFFECTION LEVEL	● ●
FRIENDLINESS TOWARD OTHER DOGS	●
FRIENDLINESS TOWARD OTHER PETS	● ● ●
FRIENDLINESS TOWARD STRANGERS	●
FRIENDLINESS TOWARD CHILDREN	●
EASE OF TRAINING	● ●
GROOMING REQUIREMENTS	● ● ●
SHEDDING	● ● ●
SPACE REQUIREMENTS	●
OK FOR BEGINNERS	● ●

4 dots = highest rating

Affectionate Poms are affectionate, but on their terms. Your Pom's affectionate nature is more likely to surface once he's had a chance to dissipate some of that abundant energy (*Why stop to snuggle when there are so many other things to do?*). He'll probably be quite devoted to your entire family, but he may become particularly attached to one special person.

Playful Poms are fun-loving and playful, eagerly joining in games wherever they can find them—or making them up if necessary. Your Pom's favorite playmate will be, of course, you.

Athletic Many people are surprised to learn that Poms are quite athletic, thanks to their working-dog ancestry. When you're looking for activities to share with your Pom, don't bypass ones that require athletic ability, such as Frisbee or agility tasks.

Intelligent Poms are thinking dogs, with minds that work all the time scoping out situations, looking for things to do, taking stock of what's going on. To keep your Pom happy and out of trouble, you'll need to make sure he has plenty of mental exercise as well as physical exercise. Keep his mind occupied with training (obedience, agility, and tricks) and regular exposure to new people, places, and situations.

Confident Poms are confident (some would say "cocky") dogs that are used to doing their own thinking, another trait of those working ancestors. Your Pom's confidence is the quality that makes him approach new

BE PREPARED! Ready, Set, Go!

You might be ready for a Pomeranian if . . .

- you're prepared to give him food, shelter, health care, and companionship for his entire life, which can be 15 years or even more;
- you've asked your family whether they want a dog—and they do, even if it's inconvenient at times;
- your children are at least eight years old and understand that a dog— especially a small dog—must be handled gently at all times;
- you're not allergic to dogs;
- you're ready to share your home with a dog;
- you're ready to share your life with a dog, giving him the time he needs each day, even if it means you won't have as much time for some of the other activities that you enjoy;
- you have a fenced yard or area where he can safely spend time while not in the house;
- you're ready to take the time and make the effort to train him so he's a well-mannered companion instead of a terror on paws;
- you can put up with the mess and damage that a dog can inflict on a household;
- you don't mind spending a little time every day or so brushing and grooming him (or you're willing to pay someone to do it);
- you can put up with some barking (or even a lot of barking)—most Poms have a lot to "say," and it's not always easy to train them to stop;
- you don't expect absolute obedience all the time. Poms are smart, but they've got their own opinions too; an occasional argument is a definite possibility;
- you don't expect total devotion 24/7. Your Pom will enjoy spending time with you, but he probably won't be glued to your side all day long; and
- you want a confident, intelligent companion that will entertain you even as he challenges you.

situations eagerly, but it may also lead him to argue with you when he wants to do things his way. Unfortunately, his confidence can also get him in trouble, such as when he decides to take on a dog that's much larger than he is. It's up to you to channel his confidence into productive—and safe— activities.

Watchdog Pomeranians got their watchdog abilities from their Spitz ancestors, so your pal is genetically programmed to sound the alarm if he sees anything amiss. If he carries the barking to an extreme, you'll need to teach him to alert you, then stop on your command. And don't expect his watchdogging to go beyond barking—he's not likely to attack an intruder.

Pomeranian Pros and Cons

Pomeranians have a lot of good points, but like all dogs, they're got some bad points too. Some of these features are universal to small dogs, but others are more Pom-specific. Either way, knowing these pros and cons can help you decide if a Pomeranian is the right dog for you.

Pros

- Poms are less expensive to feed, board, and medicate than larger dogs.
- They don't need big treats for big chewing fun.
- They produce smaller "piles," which means less cleanup for you.
- They don't need big carriers or crates, so it's easier to take them places.
- At just 3 to 7 pounds (1–3 kg), Poms easily meet the size limitations for places like hotels.
- They don't need much space in the yard or the house.
- It's easy to meet their exercise requirements.
- They don't drag you around on the leash.

Cons

- Poms can be easily injured if they jump off furniture, or you drop or step on them.
- If they get underfoot, they can easily trip you.
- They're not suitable companions for children who play roughly.
- They can be killed or injured by some animals (for example, larger dogs or predators, including some birds).
- They need regular coat care.
- Some Poms bark excessively.

Chapter Two

The Mind of the Pomeranian

That fluffy Pomeranian sleeping by your feet may appear thoroughly domesticated, but he's closer to his wild relatives than you might think. Learning about his "wild side" will help you communicate with him and better understand his behavior.

Life in the Pack

Wolves are social animals, living and interacting with other wolves in an extended family group called a pack. The wolf pack lives within a specific territory; the male wolves mark the boundaries of the territory by urinating on trees, rocks, and other objects. The territory is fiercely guarded against other wolves. The pack hunts together, which is more effective than single hunting, and participates cooperatively in raising the young wolves.

The social order of the wolf pack consists of a hierarchy with one dominant (or alpha) male and other subordinate males, which may be dominant over more subordinate males. The female wolves have a similar social structure. The pack hierarchy is not constant; changes in dominance and subordinance occur relatively frequently.

Each wolf's behavior is dictated by its social rank in the pack. The alpha male eats first and chooses his mate first (usually the alpha female), and all the subordinate wolves treat him with respect (at least until someone challenges his authority). This pecking order continues all the way down to the most subordinate wolf in the pack.

Canine Body Language

Dogs and their relatives communicate through complex and sometimes subtle movements that are readily understood by other dogs. Learning to interpret canine body language will help you to better understand your Pom.

If you observe your Pom closely, you'll see examples of body language every day. The more Pom-watching you do, the better you'll become at understanding what your pal is trying to "say." You'll also notice differences

depending on the circumstances. For example, your Pom may act happy and submissive toward you, yet become more dominant (or even aggressive) around other dogs.

When it comes to happy facial expressions, some dogs go way beyond the typical mouth-open, tongue-lolling canine smile. Instead, they keep their mouths closed, wrinkle their noses, and pull their lips back to reveal their pearly-white choppers. This toothy grin can appear frighteningly similar to a snarl, but the accompanying body language (non-staring gaze, relaxed or flattened ears, relaxed posture, wagging tail) will tell you that the smiling dog is friendly or even subordinate.

Fun Facts

Almost Human

Some dogs are so "in tune" with their owners that it's easy to understand the exclamation "He thinks he's a person!" That's not exactly true, but not completely off-base either. Dogs don't have imaginations; to them other living beings are either "dog" or "not dog." So even though your Pom can't think he's a person, it's quite likely that he thinks you are a dog—an odd-looking dog, but a dog nonetheless!

HOME BASICS
Take Charge

It's easy to establish dominance with some dogs—these willing followers just tend to accept their positions. Other dogs challenge authority every chance they get. Most dogs fall somewhere in between these extremes. Use the following tactics if you need a little help convincing your Pom that you're the top dog in the family pack:

Be Aloof: Don't be too affectionate. In the canine world, subordinate pack members approach the leader and display affection instead of the other way around. Instead of picking up your Pom and petting him, call him to you and pet him only after he has obeyed a simple command, such as *sit*.

You Decide: Don't automatically respond to your Pom's every wish. As the dominant pack member, you decide when it's time to play or go outside (and you go through the door first).

Eat First: Subordinate pack members eat after the dominant ones.

Paws Off: Don't let your Pom put his paws or head in your lap when you sit down. This is a dominant behavior similar to that displayed when a dominant dog puts its front paws on the subordinate dog's back.

Pom Down: Don't allow your Pom to be physically higher than you, such as on the back of your chair or curled around your neck. These are both dominant behaviors, and if you allow them, you'll confuse your friend about his place in the family pack.

Apprehensive behavior is easy to identify but difficult to predict. If your Pom is apprehensive, he'll probably act submissive, unless he perceives that his submissive signals aren't being heeded. Even then, his first course of action will usually be escaping from whatever (or whoever) it is that scares him. If he can't get away, he may threaten to snap or bite, but never with the body language of a truly dominant aggressive dog. Dogs that become aggressive under these circumstances are often referred to as "fear biters." For more information on Pomeranian body language, see page 16.

Family Life

For a domesticated dog, the human family becomes the pack. As in the canine pack, there is one dominant member and one or more subordinate members. The territory is, of course, the home and surrounding property, although it's not unusual for a dog to decide that the pack territory also includes highly frequented areas, such as the neighborhood park.

PERSONALITY POINTERS
Pomeranian Body Language

	Head Carriage	Eyes	Ears
Friendly	Level with body or slightly elevated	Open; soft gaze	Relaxed, neither pricked forward nor flattened to head
Curious	Level with body or slightly elevated; may cock head to one side	Open, with alert gaze	Pricked forward
Excited	Elevated	Wide open; bright	Pricked forward
Playful	Elevated	Wide open; bright	Pricked forward
Dominant or Aggressive	Elevated	Wide open; direct stare	Extremely pricked forward
Anxious or Fearful	Slightly lowered or pulled back; may turn head away from object of fear	Wide open; "bug-eyed" expression; whites of eyes may show	Pulled back; may prick ears forward sporadically
Subordinate or Submissive	Slightly lowered	Partially closed; avoids eye contact	Flattened against skull

* Changes are difficult to detect because of the Pom's natural tail carriage and heavy coat.

It's important for your Pom to understand that his position in the family pack is one of subordinance to *all* humans, regardless of age or gender. This may sound harsh to you, but your Pom won't think so. Remember: In a pack all of the members know their places. If your buddy understands the social order of the family pack, he'll know how to act. If the social order constantly changes (for example, you allow dominant behavior on one day, but expect him to be subordinate on the next), he'll be confused.

Your Pomeranian and Family Members
Your Pom's relationship with each family member depends on whether he thinks that person is dominant or subordinate to him. Some dogs readily accept the husband as the dominant male, but consider the other members of the family to be subordinate. In this case, the husband has little difficulty with the dog, but the wife and children encounter varying degrees of resist-

Mouth	Body Posture	Tail
Closed or relaxed and slightly open	Upright, but relaxed	Wagging
Closed or slightly open	Alert, upright posture	Wagging or motionless
Open (teeth covered); may pant	Alert, wiggling, "bouncy"	Wagging
Closed or open with teeth exposed, lips relaxed	Wiggling; "play bow" (chest lowered, rear quarters elevated); may paw the air with front feet	Wagging
Teeth exposed, lips drawn back and tense; snarling	Tense; very forward, upright posture	Motionless; tense*
Closed; may drool if very frightened	Tense, trembling; may appear ready to flee; may release anal sac contents	Motionless; tense*
Lips pulled back; may lick or nuzzle	Crouching; may roll over on back; submissive urination	Motionless*

ance to their requests. In a variation of this behavior, the dog acknowledges both the husband and wife as dominant, but regards the children as subordinate. Neither situation is acceptable: The dog is subordinate to every human family member, even children. To remedy this behavior, the dominant family member should pay extra attention to the members treated as subordinate, which, according to canine social rules, will elevate their status. In addition, the dominant family member should ignore the dog as much as possible (still providing necessary care, of course) to reinforce the dog's subordinate status.

Sometimes a male dog treats the wife with particular deference, but treats the husband as a subordinate. In extreme cases, the dog may even threaten the husband when he approaches the wife. Such behavior indicates that the dog perceives a pair relationship with the wife and views the husband as a rival. This entirely inappropriate behavior can be thwarted without violence

by having the wife "reject" the dog by pointedly ignoring him. To reinforce the appropriate social order, the husband should assume all dog care duties until the correct status quo has been reestablished.

Pomeranians and Children

It's not unusual for a dog to regard a child as a subordinate, but it's a totally inappropriate attitude in a human household, where the dog is subordinate to all humans, even children. Some dogs display dominant behavior, such as growling at the child when she walks into the room where the dog is eating.

If your Pom is guilty of this type of behavior, you should intervene on behalf of the child, which will elevate her status in the eyes of the dog. You should also reinforce the family pack pecking order by using some of the techniques described in this chapter. Young children should never be left alone with a dog that exhibits any dominant tendencies toward them.

Some dogs seem to be somewhat confused by children and exhibit neither consistently dominant nor subordinate behavior. This frequently occurs when the dog cannot interpret the child's actions or when the child doesn't understand (or simply ignores) the behavioral language of the dog. In addition, children who are boisterous or loud may intimidate a shy, nervous dog.

Poms seem to prefer children who play gently (no tail-pulling or Pom-wrestling) and respect their canine "personal space." Even a normally quiet, friendly Pom should be constantly supervised while around young children—for the protection of the dog as well as the child. Dogs that are prone to displays of dominant behavior often cannot ever be completely trusted around children of any age.

If your Pom acts aggressively toward you, your children, or any other person, immediately seek the help of an experienced trainer or animal behaviorist. Do not try to correct this dangerous behavior problem on your own.

Your Pomeranian and Other Pets

Not surprisingly, the meeting of two dogs is accompanied by all sorts of complex social signals. How your Pom gets along with other dogs depends on many factors, such as the ages and genders of the dogs, where the meeting takes place, and whether either owner is present.

In general, dogs of different maturity stages (for example, puppies meeting adults) tend to establish an amicable relationship faster than dogs of similar maturity, unless both are puppies. Dogs of different genders also seem to accept one another more readily, although this can vary widely depending on the specific situation. For example, a female with a litter of puppies may be quite intolerant of a male dog.

Your Pom may get along better with another dog if they meet on neutral ground, away from either dog's territory. Problems can arise, however, when either (or both) of the dogs decides that a frequently visited public location, such as a park, is part of his territory. Finally, your pal may accept another dog more quickly if you and the other owner are not around to precipitate problems arising from jealousy.

Your Pom's behavior around pets other than dogs depends on both the pet and the specific situation. Despite stories to the contrary, many dogs get along quite well with cats, especially if they were raised together. In some cases, your Pom's response might depend on what the other pet is doing. For example, your buddy might get along fine with a pet rabbit that's moving around quietly, but chase it if it runs. (Some dogs and other pets, especially cats, make a game of this, but make sure both animals enjoy it.) It's best, at least at first, to constantly supervise your Pom and other pets when they are together, especially if there is a great size difference or one of the animals is capable of inflicting serious damage on the other (for example, when a Pom puppy tries to "play" with an adult cat).

Sibling Rivalry

Having two Poms can be a lot of fun, but it can give you headaches (and heartaches) when one dog picks on the other. If this sounds like the situation in your home, it's important to understand that even though both dogs should be subordinate to all human family members, they will never be social equals—one dog will always be more dominant. Canine social status isn't constant, so the top dog continually displays his dominance to keep the subordinate dog in his place. As much as possible, you should let your Poms work things out between themselves. Don't try to defend the "underdog" unless there is danger of real injury (a rare occurrence), because this will alter the social order between the dogs and ultimately cause more conflict.

Little Dog: Big Attitude

Most Poms don't seem to understand that they are little dogs. This can be a good thing—most people don't want a dog that spends all its time cowering in a corner—but it can also lead to trouble. If your Pom has a point to prove, he probably won't care that he's arguing with a dog that's more than ten times his size, but it's easy to predict who'll get hurt if the argument becomes physical. To be safe, keep your pal in a fenced yard or on a leash when you're out and about. Avoid large dogs, unless you know that they are friendly toward your Pom.

Helpful Hints

"My Pom tried to bite me when I brushed his legs!"

Your Pom may not enjoy having his legs brushed, but he needs to accept it because you're the leader. You need to remind him that he's still subordinate to you. First, teach him to obey a simple command, such as *sit* (this may take a few days). After he's learned it, have him sit while you gently brush him on part of his body where it least bothers him. Praise him when he accepts the brushing without grumbling. If he objects, stop brushing and reinforce your dominance by telling him to sit, then continue brushing. Gradually increase the extent of the brushing until he'll let you brush any part of his body. Use this technique (with adaptations if necessary) whenever your Pom needs a "refresher course" on his proper place in the family pack.

Communicating with Your Pomeranian

Scent Your Pom's sense of smell is his keenest sense (hearing is a close second). Unlike humans, who use vision to assess their environment and situation, dogs use scent. Your Pom uses his sense of smell to gain information about everything around him—what you're having for dinner, where his favorite toy is, who's at the front door. He may also "size up" another dog by sniffing the stranger's anus, genitals, mouth, and ears. (If he tries this with you, reprimand him or push him away to let him know it's unacceptable to greet humans in this fashion.) Your Pom's nose can also tell him when you're feeling stressed, anxious, or apprehensive, because changes in your body chemistry will change the way you smell, even though you may not detect it. Communication tips: Use colognes and perfumes lightly (or not at all) on yourself and your Pom, play "find the treat" (encourage your pal to find a treat hidden in your hand or pocket), give him an article of your clothing as a comfort object when he's at the boarding kennel or veterinary clinic, and keep your "cool" when faced with stressful situations, so your buddy will stay calm too.

Hearing Your Pom hears lower-pitched sounds just about as well as you do, but that's where the similarity ends. When it comes to mid-range sounds, he can detect them about four times farther away than you can. And your pal's hearing is even better in the high-frequency range: the upper limit for people is about 23,000 Hertz; for a dog, it's 46,000 Hertz, which is why your Pom can easily hear a "silent" dog whistle and you can't. There's never any need to shout at your buddy. If his hearing is normal, shouting at him would be like someone blasting you with a huge set of speakers turned all the way up. He'll probably hear you perfectly even if you whisper. If your Pom is a senior with some hearing loss, he may hear you better if you speak loudly (without shouting) in a lower-pitched voice. Communication tips: Talk to your Pom, use his name frequently, alter the volume of your voice from a whisper to normal volume, alter your tone to express pleasure or displeasure (for example, firm for commands, happy for praise or play), and sing.

Sight Your Pom's vision isn't nearly as acute as his senses of smell and hearing. His retina contains mostly rods (light-sensitive cells that provide motion detection and vision in dim light), so he readily detects small movements and sees better in the dark than you do. A lack of retinal cones (cells responsible for color perception and visual acuity) means your pal doesn't see colors or details very well. He's not totally color-blind; he can discern blue-violet, yellow, and various shades of gray, but can't tell the difference between red, yellow, orange, and green. Despite these limitations, your Pom's vision is an important tool that he constantly uses, often in conjunction with the other senses, to interpret the body language of other dogs and humans. Communication tips: Convey your mood by your body posture (for example, "take charge" by standing tall, initiate play by taking a playful stance), and teach hand signals in conjunction with obedience commands.

Touch Dogs are "contact" animals: They like to be touched by each other and by their humans. Your Pom's individual preferences depend on his personality and the type of contact, such as cuddling, petting, or scratching. He undoubtedly has some favorite touch spots (for example, behind the ears) and some that aren't so favorite (for example, paws). Communication tips: Substitute ear scratches or petting for edible rewards, groom your Pom, allow him to sit close to you (at your choice, not his), and use stroking or massage to calm him when he's upset.

Taste The canine sense of taste is rather poor, which is probably why some dogs, given the chance, will eat almost anything. This deficiency is caused by a lack of taste buds—dogs have only about one-sixth the number of them that humans do. Like most animals, your Pom has tastes he likes and those he doesn't. He may be more willing to taste unusual foods (for example, raw vegetables) if he sees you enjoying them. Communication tips: Offer edible treats as special rewards, and occasionally share tidbits of healthful "people food."

Chapter Three

How to Choose a Pomeranian

You've studied the dog books, gone to the dog shows, talked with your dog-owning friends, and finally, you've made up your mind: You want a Pomeranian.

Congratulations! You're about to embark on a wonderful adventure. Just remember that owning a dog isn't all fun and games (though you'll certainly have plenty of those with a Pom); it's a huge responsibility. You'll need to give your Pom food, shelter, grooming, veterinary care, love, and companionship for the rest of his life. If you're ready for that kind of commitment, then let's start Pom-shopping!

Pomeranian Choices

You know you want a Pom, but do you know what kind of Pom you want? There are lots of choices: pet Poms, show Poms, puppies, adults, males, or females—and that doesn't even count all the different colors!

You don't have to decide on everything before you go shopping, but it's a good idea to have a list of Pom "must haves" and "definitely nots." That way you won't come home with a puppy, when you really wanted an adult, or a show-quality dog, when pet-quality was more what you (and your wallet) had in mind.

Pet Pom or Show Pom?

First and foremost, your Pom will be a pet. If this isn't the main reason why you want a dog, then perhaps you should rethink your decision to get one. Dogs need human companionship; they shouldn't be kept solely as show or breeding animals, isolated from their people.

That said, it's okay to have a Pom that's a pet as well as a show animal. In fact, most successful show dogs are also pets. If you don't intend to show your Pom in conformation shows, however, there's no need to pay big bucks for a show-quality dog. Plenty of Poms aren't suitable for conformation showing simply because they don't have the necessary physical characteristics. There's nothing wrong with them, they just don't typify what the

perfect Pom should look like—that is, the AKC breed standard. Your Pom doesn't have to be beautiful to be a terrific pet, as long as he's got a good temperament. Besides, even if he doesn't quite measure up to the breed standard, you can still show him in competitions such as obedience trials or agility trials, where performance is the only thing that counts.

If you decide that you'd like to show in conformation dog shows, you'll need to purchase the best Pom you can afford, without compromising temperament for physical perfection. A show-quality Pom usually has parents that have had successful show careers, but that doesn't necessarily mean that a puppy will follow in his parents' paw prints. A knowledgeable Pom breeder can help you select a show-quality puppy, but keep in mind that even experts sometimes find it difficult to pick a future winner. It's a little easier (and usually more expensive) to pick a show-quality adult, but you should still enlist the help of an experienced breeder.

Puppy or Adult?

Now you need to decide whether you want to adopt your Pomeranian as a puppy or an adult. There are advantages either way. What you decide depends on your expectations, your physical capabilities, your anticipated time commitment, and even your family's preference. For instance, a 23-year-old single woman may prefer a puppy, whereas a retired couple may feel more comfortable with an adult.

FYI: Pros and Cons of Puppies and Adults

	PUPPY	ADULT
Appearance	Cute!	Cute!
Personality	Friendly, trusting, affectionate, curious.	Usually calmer and more "settled." May be more confident or even assertive.
Bonding	Quickly bonds with caregiver.	May be slow to bond with new owner. May have developed preference for certain people (for example, adults or females).
Socialization	Ongoing in puppies <12 weeks old.	Already socialized; socialization may be satisfactory or poor.
Background	Background and medical history usually known.	Background and medical history may be questionable or unknown, especially with rescues.
Independence	Needs constant supervision. Shouldn't be left alone for long periods.	Requires less supervision. Can be left alone for longer periods of time.
Behavior	Very active, curious ("into everything"). Chewing is common, especially while teething.	Still active, but explores less. Doesn't chew as much. May have developed undesirable behaviors or habits.
Housetraining	Usually not housetrained.	Varies from inadequate to excellent.
Other Training	None. Must consider short attention span when training.	Varies from none to extensive. Longer attention span may make training easier; more independent nature may make it more difficult.
Adult Qualities	Difficult to assess.	Adult personality and physical traits already present.

Male or Female?

If you're like a lot of people, you probably have in mind which gender of Pom you want. That doesn't mean you have to be locked in to that choice—there are good points and not-so-good points about both males and females. You may find that your "perfect Pom" is not at all what you thought you wanted, at least when it comes to gender!

You don't have to decide whether you want a male or female before you go dog-shopping, but it helps to know the pros and cons of each. At least that way you'll know what to expect if your determination to select one gender gets derailed by a particularly appealing Pom of the opposite sex!

A female Pomeranian comes into "heat" (estrus) about twice a year. During this time, she must be kept away from male dogs to avoid an unwanted litter of puppies. Females in proestrus (the time just prior to actual "heat") have a bloody vaginal discharge that may stain carpets and furniture.

Male dogs tend to be somewhat more aggressive than females, but this varies a lot, depending on the individual. Pomeranians aren't usually aggressive toward people, but they aren't afraid to "stand up" to other dogs much larger than themselves. Males tend to roam more, looking for females in heat and marking their territory by urinating on upright objects such as trees and telephone poles. Marking behavior in the house isn't usually a problem, as long as the dog has been reliably housetrained.

Most gender-related problems can be remedied by spaying or neutering. If you want to show your Pom in conformation shows, however, spaying or neutering isn't an option since only intact dogs can compete in this type of show. Spayed and neutered dogs can be shown in other types of competition, such as obedience trials and agility trials.

Pom Sources

Now that you've thought a bit about the kind of Pom you want, it's time to start looking for your new best friend. Poms are popular, so you probably won't have any trouble finding one for sale. However, don't make the mistake of buying just any Pom. Look for the right Pom, one that's healthy and well-socialized, with a personality that complements your own. Finding this kind of Pom will take some time and effort.

Breeders

For selection and quality, your best source for a new puppy or dog is a reputable Pomeranian breeder. These dedicated individuals strive to improve the Pomeranian breed by breeding the best dogs possible. Because their reputation depends on the dogs that they breed and sell, breeders work hard to provide their puppies with proper nutrition, socialization, and health care. In addition, the professional breeder maintains complete records—registration papers, pedigree, show record, health record, and so on—for each dog. Reputable breeders are very selective about the dogs they breed, so they may have only a few puppies and/or adult dogs available (beware of the breeder who has dozens), or they may have none at all.

Prices vary, depending on age and quality—for example, a pet-quality puppy will cost less than a show-quality adult. A reputable breeder tries to match the right dog or puppy to just the right owner. Breeders are also an invaluable source of information for new owners both at the time of purchase and afterward.

If you'd like to extend your search for the perfect Pomeranian to the world beyond your immediate area, check the breeder listings in dog magazines, such as the *AKC Gazette*, *Dog Fancy*, or *Dog World*, or search the Internet. The Internet, in particular, offers a wide variety of breeder websites, which often contain detailed information about the breeding program, photographs or videos of puppies and their parents, and even helpful hints about living with a Pom.

Helpful Hints

Finding a Breeder

Check the following sources to find a Pomeranian breeder in your area:

The American Pomeranian Club: Their website has a directory of breeders, listed by state.

Local Dog Clubs: Members of an all-breed club may be able to recommend a local Pomeranian breeder. In some areas, you may be lucky enough to find a dog club devoted solely to Poms.

Veterinarians and Groomers: These professionals often know local breeders.

Pet Supply Stores: Talk to the store personnel and scout their bulletin board (if they have one) for breeder ads.

Newspaper Ads: This may be hit or miss. Some reputable breeders advertise in newspapers; others never do, preferring "word-of-mouth" advertising instead.

Many prospective owners don't consider searching nationwide because they don't want to select a dog or puppy from photos or videos, then have it shipped to them. Others feel comfortable using this method, especially if they know the breeder or they're reasonably certain that the breeder will have the perfect Pom for them. Even if you don't plan to make a long-distance purchase, it might be worth it to contact a distant breeder; he or she may know someone in your area who raises Poms.

Rescue Organizations

Pomeranian rescue organizations help find good homes for Poms that have been rescued from shelters or abusive homes, or given up by owners who can no longer care for them. The rescued Poms are evaluated for health status and temperament, vaccinated, and spayed or neutered before they're offered for adoption.

Adopting a dog from a rescue organization isn't for everyone. Most rescue dogs are adults, so if you're looking for a puppy, you'll probably have to go somewhere else. Complete information about the dog's background and health status may not be available. Thorough post-rescue evaluation and health care

helps minimize potential problems. Some rescue dogs need behavior modification or rehabilitation. The amount needed (or whether it's needed at all) varies, depending on the individual dog and the rescue situation.

If you think you'd like to adopt a rescued Pom, contact the American Pomeranian Club to find a rescue organization near you. Some have websites with adoption information, which may include pictures of available dogs. Don't expect that you'll just be able to show up and pick out your Pom; it doesn't happen that way—rescue groups carefully screen prospective owners and counsel them about Pomeranian ownership. After adoption, they usually continue to assist the owner throughout the Pom's lifetime. Many rescue operations allow the owner to return a dog he or she can no longer care for.

Animal Shelters

There is one compelling reason to adopt a Pomeranian from an animal shelter: You may be saving his life. No-kill shelters have become more common in recent years, but sadly, many shelters still euthanize unwanted pets after a certain time period because they can't afford to keep them. Adoption fees at shelters are usually quite reasonable and often include spaying or neutering (which virtually all shelters require before an animal can be adopted), and sometimes vaccination and microchipping.

Unfortunately, adopting a dog from a shelter has some significant disadvantages. Background and medical history may be unknown or sketchy at best. It may also be difficult to accurately evaluate the dog's temperament in the shelter environment. In addition, most shelters are chronically short of both funding and staff members, so often little is done to assist adopters either before or after adoption.

Despite the disadvantages, thousands of dogs are successfully adopted from animal shelters each year. So go ahead and look; just remember the limitations associated with this source.

Choosing a Puppy

Once you've done all your homework, it's time to pick out your Pomeranian. Choosing a puppy is especially fun, but it can be very difficult to make up your mind—Pom puppies are so cute, you'll probably want them all! You can probably narrow the field a little if you know what to look for.

The ideal age to adopt a puppy is between eight and twelve weeks. Puppies this age are usually weaned (if not, look elsewhere), eating well, and very energetic. They usually adapt quickly to their new home and form strong attachments to their new human family.

When you arrive at the breeder's home, take a minute to look around. Are the premises neat and clean? Do the puppies have a safe, fenced yard to play in? Do the puppies and other dogs look healthy and well cared for? If the answer to all these questions is yes, go ahead and look at the puppies.

CHECKLIST

Puppy Health Check

✔ **General Behavior/Symptoms:** alert, active, wiggly, and curious; no vomiting, sneezing, coughing, or wheezing.

✔ **Body Condition:** "rounded" but not excessively fat or potbellied.

✔ **Coat:** thick and soft, with no bare spots.

✔ **Skin:** no sores, rashes, or inflammation; no fleas or ticks.

✔ **Nose:** no discharge.

✔ **Gums:** pink, not red or pale.

✔ **Eyes:** clear, no discharge; eyelids should not turn in or out.

✔ **Ears:** no discharge, no itchiness.

✔ **Abdomen:** no umbilical hernia (a small soft swelling near the puppy's "belly button").

✔ **Scrotum (males):** both testicles should be in the scrotum by 12 weeks of age.

✔ **Anal Area:** clean and dry, with no signs of irritation.

Note: Even if you don't find any problems, make the sale contingent on the puppy receiving a "clean bill of health" from your veterinarian within two or three days.

If, however, you find unkempt, dirty facilities and unhealthy dogs, do your puppy-shopping somewhere else.

It's only natural to want to meet the puppies right away, but before you do, take some time to find out a little more about them. (If you don't do it before you meet the youngsters, you might forget what you were going to ask.) In particular, ask the breeder about the following:

- **Health Care:** The puppies should have had their first immunizations and should have been dewormed. The breeder should also be able to tell you if the puppy you're considering has had any illnesses or injuries.
- **Temperament:** A breeder who has evaluated each puppy's temperament and personality will be better able to help you pick out your new best friend.
- **Socialization:** Responsible breeders work diligently to make sure their puppies are well-socialized and comfortable around people.
- **Parents:** Meeting the puppy's sire (father) and dam (mother) can give you a good idea of how your baby Pom will look and act as an adult.
- **Information and Advice:** A responsible breeder doesn't mind answering questions at the time of purchase—or anytime after.
- **Contingency Plans:** Find out if the breeder will take your Pom back if you can't keep him. Responsible breeders want their dogs to have good homes, even if they have to take one back. It's better than having the dog end up in an animal shelter or abandoned.
- **References:** The breeder should be able to give you the names and phone numbers of previous buyers.

Finally, it's time to meet the puppies. When the breeder shows them to you, take a minute to observe them by themselves. Are they active and playful? Do any of them seem reluctant to join in? Are any of the puppies noticeably smaller than the others?

Next, get down on your knees and call the puppies over to you, talking in a high-pitched voice and patting your knees. You should have a lapful of baby Poms almost immediately. Don't consider any puppy that doesn't come running to you. Carefully look over the others. Do any of them seem timid or nervous? These shy puppies might thrive with the right handling, but cross them off your list.

Your best choice will be a healthy, active puppy that's sociable and outgoing. To find this special little Pom, you'll need to carefully assess the health and personality of each puppy you're considering. Don't forget to get the breeder's input too.

Puppy Aptitude Testing

Puppy aptitude testing (PAT) was originally developed more than 50 years ago as a way to evaluate a puppy's potential as a guide dog. Since that time, it's been adapted for use in companion dogs. Many breeders and prospective owners use PAT to assess temperament and personality in an effort to find a puppy that best suits the owner's skill levels and experience.

Ideally, PAT should be conducted under the following conditions:

- The puppy should be tested as close as possible to the age of 49 days.
- The testing should take place in a place that is unfamiliar to the puppy, such as a room where the puppy hasn't been.
- The puppy should not know the tester.
- No other dogs should be present during the testing.
- The puppy should be tested before being fed, when he is alert and lively.
- The puppy should not be tested if he has been vaccinated within the past 24 hours or if he seems to be ill.
- Only the first response is evaluated.

PERSONALITY POINTERS
Puppy Aptitude Testing

Test	What to Do
Social Attraction	Coax the puppy toward you from about 4 feet (1.2 m) away.
Following	Walk away, encouraging the puppy to follow you.
Restraint	Gently roll the puppy on his back and hold him there for 30 seconds.
Social Dominance	Stroke the puppy on his back while he sits or stands.
Elevation Dominance	Gently lift the puppy about 2 feet (60 cm) off the ground and hold him there for 30 seconds.
Retrieving	Throw a crumpled-up paper about 4 feet (1.2 m) away and encourage the puppy to retrieve it.
Touch Sensitivity	Squeeze the webbing between the puppy's toes, gradually increasing pressure.
Sound Sensitivity	Make a sharp noise several feet away from the puppy.
Sight Sensitivity	Jerk a towel on a string along the floor about 2 feet (60 cm) away from the puppy.
Stability	Open an umbrella about 5 feet (1.5 m) away from the puppy and place it on the floor.

Experts recommend using a tester, who administers the test, and a scorer, who scores the responses (from 1 to 6) without disturbing the puppy. You don't have to do it that way—it's okay to test the puppy and simply evaluate the responses yourself. You won't have a bunch of numerical scores to analyze, but you'll still learn a lot about the puppy you're considering.

Choosing an Adult

Choosing an adult Pom is a little bit different—and in some ways a little easier—than choosing a puppy. Since the dog you're considering is "all grown up," the breeder can provide valuable information about everything from temperament and sociability to training and show experience, if any. In addition to asking some of the same questions listed above about puppies, also inquire about the adult's background and socialization; personality

The Puppy Should . . .	The Puppy Shouldn't . . .
Readily approach you, tail down.	Jump up and bite at your hands. Ignore you.
Readily follow you, tail down.	Get underfoot and bite at your feet. Ignore you.
Settle after only a little struggling.	Struggle vigorously and try to bite. Go limp, while avoiding eye contact.
Accept the stroking, squirm, and lick your hands.	Jump, growl, or try to bite. Move away and stay away.
Accept the positioning without struggling and remain relaxed.	Struggle vigorously and try to bite. Freeze without struggling.
Chase the paper and return to you, with or without it.	Chase the paper and run away with it. Ignore the paper.
Pull away neither extremely quickly nor extremely slowly.	Pull away very slowly. Pull away very quickly.
Listen and locate the sound.	Listen, locate the sound, and run toward it, barking. Ignore the sound.
Watch with curiosity, tail down.	Attack the towel. Hide from the towel.
Sit and look at the umbrella, but not move toward it.	Run to the umbrella, then bite or mouth it. Run away from the umbrella.

and disposition (easygoing, nervous, affectionate, cranky); home environment (home, kennel, indoors/outdoors etc.); training, including housetraining; experience with children, other dogs, and other pets; best qualities; and worst qualities.

Before you greet your prospective new friend, watch the way he interacts with the breeder. Is he outgoing and responsive, or does he just go his own way? When the two of you are introduced, watch his body language. He may not bounce up and down with joy to see you (although that would be a definite plus in his favor), but he should be obviously friendly. Don't even consider him if he shows any signs of dominant or aggressive behavior. If he's a little timid when you first meet, give him some time to "warm up" to you. If he doesn't, pass him up.

Next, observe how the Pom responds to you. Pet him (try to find his favorite itchy spots), and then encourage him to follow you around. He should respond willingly and happily. Next, pick him up and check him out—

handle his paws, examine his ears, look in his mouth. If he lets you do this without protesting, he gets extra points. If he's obviously nervous, he may just need a little more time to get to know you, so make an appointment with the breeder for a second visit. If he's still nervous on the second visit, cross him off your list.

Since adult dogs are more "set in their ways" than puppies, the breeder may let you take your prospective Pom home on a trial basis. This is a good way to see how the dog will act in a different setting, around different people. If the breeder doesn't allow home trials, make another appointment (or even more) if you need more time to reach a decision. Don't hesitate to ask for more time—a responsible breeder won't pressure you to adopt a Pom that you're uncertain about.

Understanding Registration

A registered Pomeranian is one that has a registration certificate ("papers") issued by the American Kennel Club (AKC) or another registry such as the Canadian Kennel Club or the United Kennel Club. Since the AKC registers the largest numbers of dogs, the following information summarizes their registration rules.

When an AKC-registered dog has puppies, the breeder (the dog's owner) registers the litter. The breeder is the only person who can do this. When you buy a puppy that is part of a registered litter, the breeder must give you the puppy's individual registration application or, if the breeder has already registered the individual puppy, its registration certificate. If the puppy doesn't have a registration certificate, you must get the registration application from the breeder if you want to register the puppy; the AKC registers only dogs that are members of registered litters.

The individual registration application will include the puppy's gender, color and markings, registration type (full, limited, or conditional), your name and address, and the breeder's signature. You'll provide the name you've chosen for your puppy, and payment information, and make some optional choices (for example, whether you'd like to purchase your puppy's pedigree). Then you sign the form and send it to the AKC. You can also register a dog online at the AKC's website (*www.akc.org*). After a few weeks, you'll receive your puppy's registration certificate.

Your Pom's registration certificate will contain his name and registration number, the names of his sire and dam and their registration numbers, a description (breed, gender, color, and date of birth), his breeder's name, and his owner's name (you!). Some dogs' registration certificates also contain other information, if applicable, such as certification numbers for registries (for example, Orthopedic Foundation for Animals [OFA] and Canine Eye Registry Foundation [CERF]) or notation of DNA profile. The certificate's border color indicates whether your puppy's registration is full (purple border), limited (orange border), or conditional (yellow border).

If your Pom has limited registration, it means that he's purebred, but his offspring cannot be registered. Breeders use limited registration to keep owners from breeding pet-quality dogs that lack the qualities needed to improve the breed. The litter owner (usually the breeder) is the only person who can decide whether a puppy should have full or limited registration and the only one who can change the registration status from limited to full. Dogs with limited registration can't be shown in conformation dog shows, but they can participate in all other AKC events.

A dog with conditional registration is one that is recognized as purebred, but its pedigree cannot be completely verified by DNA profiling. The offspring of conditionally registered dogs cannot receive full registration, only conditional registration. Dogs with conditional registration can compete in all AKC events, except conformation shows and field trials. A dog's registration can be changed from conditional to full if DNA profiling verifies parentage for at least three generations.

It's important to realize that a registration certificate is proof of a dog's breed and parentage, but it doesn't guarantee his quality. That's okay—you probably already know that your Pom will be a champion best friend!

Time to Go

Once you've chosen your Pom pal, all that's left to do is settle on a price (most likely, you and the breeder have already discussed this) and any conditions of the sale, such as whether you have the right to return the puppy if he doesn't pass a veterinary exam. Ideally, the terms of the sale will be clearly spelled out in a contract. You'll also need to obtain the puppy's registration application from the breeder. The breeder may also give you written instructions and other information about caring for your new Pom.

The breeder will probably want to remain in contact with you after the sale so he or she can keep track of how you and your new friend are doing. If you plan to show your Pom, the breeder will definitely want to be updated, since show ring success reflects well on the breeding program as well as the dog.

Finally, you've wrapped up all the official business, so it's time to take your brand new Pomeranian home. Be sure to put your new pal in a carrier for the car ride—it's a lot safer for both of you. Don't make the trip in silence; talk to your little pal. It will reassure him if he's a little nervous about riding in the car; plus it's a good way for the two of you to get better acquainted.

Chapter Four

Caring for a Puppy

Y ou've adopted a Pomeranian puppy! You're undoubtedly excited, but you may be feeling a little nervous too, especially if you've never owned a puppy before. That's understandable; after all, your puppy will depend on you for food, shelter, health care, and companionship for the rest of his life. It might seem a little overwhelming right now, but you and your little Pom pal are going to have a lot of fun together.

Pom Ages and Stages

Your Pom puppy will do a lot of growing and developing in his first year of life. Knowing a little bit about the stages of puppy development will help you understand your youngster right now and let you know what to expect in the months to come.

Neonatal Period

During the neonatal period (birth to two weeks of age), the puppy relies on his mother for everything. Virtually everything he does at this stage is governed by reflex—pain avoidance, suckling, righting (rolling onto his abdomen after being placed on his side), and urinating and defecating when his mother licks his urogenital area. His eyes and ears are closed at birth, but usually open by about two weeks of age.

CAUTION

Your puppy may not be fully protected by his vaccinations until he's 16 to 20 weeks old. If he's younger than this, you should allow contact only with healthy, vaccinated dogs. Don't take him to the park or any other area frequented by dogs, because he could be exposed to distemper, parvovirus, and other diseases.

Transitional Period

During the transitional period (two to three weeks of age), the puppy's physical and mental development proceeds rapidly. He crawls, urinates, and defecates on his own. Vision is normal by three to four weeks of age. Toward the end of this period, the puppy begins to socialize with his littermates and mother.

Socialization Period

During the socialization period (three to twelve weeks of age), the puppy starts walking, climbing, and eating solid and liquid food. Socialization peaks at about six to eight weeks and starts to diminish at twelve weeks. Early on, the puppy socializes primarily with his littermates and mother. Some puppies start interacting with humans as early as five weeks of age, and most interact eagerly with humans by seven to eight weeks of age. During this period, the puppy is especially receptive to new stimuli, experiences, and individuals, but he may also be easily frightened. If this happens, it will probably have long-lasting effects.

Helpful Hints

Early Handling

Early on, get your Pom puppy used to being examined and handled; regularly look in his mouth, check his ears, handle his paws, clip his nails (or pretend to, if they don't need it), and look under his tail. Later, if he has a problem that you need to check out and/or treat, he'll be more likely to cooperate. He'll be a better patient for your veterinarian too.

Juvenile Period

During the juvenile period, which extends from 12 weeks until the onset of sexual maturity (as early as 24 weeks in Poms and other small dogs), the puppy continues to develop physically and mentally. Adult behaviors emerge and become established during this period. Undesirable behaviors, such as jumping up, nipping, chewing, and rowdiness, can become major problems as the puppy becomes more independent and less accepting of correction. It's not unusual for mental maturity to occur later than physical maturity; many dogs still act like puppies long after they've matured physically.

Socialization

Your Pom puppy needs to be properly socialized so he learns how to interact appropriately with humans and other dogs. If this doesn't occur, he could develop into a timid, fearful, or even aggressive adult. Puppies already exhibiting some of these traits (ideally, yours isn't one of them) are particularly prone to developing serious behavior problems if deprived of adequate socialization.

The "window of opportunity" for socialization is relatively narrow, starting around three weeks of age, peaking at six to eight weeks, and starting to decline at about twelve weeks. During this time, puppies need to be exposed to as many socialization experiences as possible, including socialization with people they don't know and dogs they don't know. They also need plenty of auditory, visual, and tactile experiences, plus generous amounts of interaction with their owners.

So how do you go about socializing your little friend? Expose him to all different types of individuals (humans, dogs, and other animals), situations, and experiences. Some experts use a procedure called the "Rule of Sevens," in which the puppy, by the time he's seven weeks old, has had these experiences:

- Walked or played on seven different surfaces.
- Played with seven different types of objects.
- Been in seven different locations.
- Attempted seven different challenges (for example, climbed steps or gone through a tunnel).
- Eaten from seven different containers.
- Eaten in seven different locations.
- Heard seven different sounds.
- Met and played with seven new people, including children and senior adults.

You may not be able to follow this plan to the letter (it may be impossible, if your baby Pom was older than seven weeks when you adopted him). Still, it's important to give him as many socialization experiences as possible, preferably during that socialization "window of opportunity" when he'll benefit most from them.

In a perfect world, your puppy's socialization would proceed smoothly and quickly. But this is real life, not a perfect world, so there may be times when your little pal just isn't interested in your socialization efforts. Maybe he's tired, in which case he needs a nap, not socialization. Maybe he's over-whelmed by too many new experiences in one day. If so, take a break and try again tomorrow. Maybe he's scared—of whatever you're doing (for example, making a loud noise) or just of everything in general. For unknown reasons, many puppies have times within the peak socialization period when they're easily frightened. If your little one is wide-eyed and nervous, stop what you're doing, reassure him, and switch to a fun, non-scary activity.

Basic Necessities

It's fun to look at all the dog stuff at the pet supply store, even if you don't own a dog. Now that you've adopted a Pom, though, you've got the perfect reason to buy some of those things that you've admired for so long.

First of all, your little friend needs a food dish and a water bowl or bottle. Feeding equipment doesn't have to be fancy or expensive, just functional. A wide-based bowl made of crockery, plastic, or stainless steel can be used for food or water. Crockery bowls work well because they can't be tipped over as easily as ones made of plastic or stainless steel. Some stores carry suction-footed racks for food and water bowls. Water bottles that mount on the side of a crate or exercise pen are especially useful, but make sure your Pom knows how to drink out of it.

You'll also need to buy a carrier or crate for your puppy's indoor bed. Carriers, which are constructed of molded plastic, are useful for car travel or transport. Wire mesh crates are convenient because they can be raised up on wooden blocks or rails, which will allow urine to drain out if the puppy

has an "accident" in the carrier. Some crates are portable. A mesh floor isn't as comfortable as a solid floor, but your Pom probably won't mind as long as he has a soft cushion or blanket to sleep on. If you choose a carrier, you may be able to purchase a mesh floor for it. Choose a crate or carrier that's big enough for your little pal to easily stand up and turn around in, but not so big that he can eliminate in one end and sleep in the other. To save money, buy an adult-sized crate or carrier and put in a partition that you can remove when your puppy needs more space.

Exercise pens (ex-pens) aren't essential equipment, but they're useful when you need to confine your Pom. They're portable, easy to set up and take down (inside or outside), and most have a modular construction so you can make them larger. If you decide to get an ex-pen for your Pom, make sure it's at least 2½ feet (75 cm) high.

Finally, you'll need to get a collar for your new little friend. Don't get a fancy one right now, because he'll soon outgrow it. A simple buckle-on nylon collar will work just fine. Choose a leash that's made of nylon web or leather, not chain, which could hurt your pal if it flips across his face or gets wrapped around a leg.

Toys

A puppy can have fun with almost anything, regardless of whether it's a puppy toy or not. Of course, you might have a problem with this attitude when your youngster starts "playing" with your shoes, clothing, or furniture. Playing with these makeshift non-toys isn't just aggravating (and expensive, in some cases), but can be downright dangerous for your pal if he invents games like "swallow the string" or "eat the electrical cord."

Providing your Pom with an assortment of fun, puppy-safe toys will keep him from amusing himself with these destructive and potentially dangerous activities.

When it comes to dog toys, there are two basic types: chew toys and chase toys. (Sometimes these functions overlap.) Most of the other features, such

FYI: Rawhide: Yes or No?

Rawhide items provide a lot of chewing enjoyment, but they must be used safely. Rawhide is digestible if it's well-chewed into small pieces, but some dogs gulp down large chunks, which could lodge in the esophagus, stomach, or intestines and cause obstruction.

Digestive tract obstruction isn't the only risk associated with rawhide. Although these products are tough and dry when new, excessive chewing makes them soft and soggy. The soft, moist rawhide fosters the growth of many types of bacteria, including *E. coli* and *Salmonella*, which can be hazardous for your Pom (and you, if you handle the bacteria-laden rawhide).

Take these precautions to keep your little friend safe while he enjoys his rawhide:

- Give him a large chew, not one that he can gulp down in a few bites.
- If he tries to wolf down chunks of his rawhide bone, give him thin strips, which he can chew up into small, harmless pieces.
- Supervise him while he's chewing on a rawhide toy.
- If he starts biting off big chunks of rawhide, give him a larger chew or a toy made of a different material. Don't give him bones: They're more dangerous than rawhide.
- Don't leave the rawhide toy on the floor or in the yard, where it could get dirty.
- If the toy gets soggy, take it away and let it dry out before giving it back to your buddy.
- If your Pom gnaws his rawhide chew down to a size that he can swallow, confiscate it and throw it away.

as squeakers, bells, and clever shapes, are simply embellishments, which often seem to appeal primarily to the owner, not the dog. Some of these can even be dangerous. For example, if your Pom chews a squeaker or bell out of a toy, he could wind up choking on it or suffering a digestive tract obstruction.

Other types of toys that could be hazardous for your Pom include

- toys made of wood, hard plastic, or other splintery materials;
- toys that can be swallowed (for example, small balls, marbles, and other small objects);
- toys that shred into strings, threads, or fabric pieces (for example, rope toys, fabric toys, toys made with yarn or string);
- ropes, cords, or anything else that presents a strangling hazard; and
- balls that are small enough to lodge in the back of the throat (for this reason, always bounce a ball to your pal instead of throwing it directly to him).

Stuffable Toys These are chew toys with cavities that can be filled with treats or food and are popular with dogs of all ages. Understandably, a toy stuffed with food usually holds a dog's interest longer than a conventional toy (few things are more interesting to a dog than food). If you're going to be away from home for a while, you can put a meal-size portion of food in the toy; your Pom will stay busy trying to get every last piece of food, which will keep him from getting bored. Keep track of the food or treats you put in the stuffable toy, so you don't overfeed your little friend.

Chew Bones You can also find various types of natural and artificial chew bones at your pet supply store. Some of these are entire beef bones, which have been specially processed and smoked for added scent and flavor. Some pet supply stores also carry dried cattle hooves, which are very popular with dogs. Nonedible artificial chew bones, which are made of nylon, rubber, or other materials that have been treated to appeal to dogs, provide the satisfaction of bone-chewing without any of the dangers. Edible artificial chew bones can be eaten without ill effects.

The Pom-House

If your youngster will eventually spend more than a few minutes outside (for instance, during the day while you're at work), he'll need a doghouse. Doghouses are available at retail outlets, such as pet supply stores, hardware stores, and discount stores, but you can also build one if you're handy with tools. Don't forget to check the ads in the newspaper or other local publications—you may find a high-quality doghouse at a bargain price.

The ideal doghouse should be roomy enough that your pal can stand up and turn around in it; leak-proof, for protection during bad weather; and insulated for winter warmth, if necessary.

Feeding Your Puppy

Puppies have nutritional needs that are different from those of adult dogs. For instance, your Pom puppy has a higher metabolic rate than an adult Pom, so he requires more calories per pound of body weight. He also needs more protein to support his rapid growth and development. His diet must contain the correct balance of calcium and phosphorus, minerals that are essential for proper development of his bones and teeth.

You can meet all of your youngster's nutritional requirements by feeding him a completely balanced commercial puppy food. If you choose a completely balanced puppy food, you won't need to supplement your baby Pom's diet with additional meat, milk, eggs, or vitamins.

If you don't know if a food is completely balanced, check the label; the manufacturer can't make that claim unless the food meets certain nutritional standards. Puppy foods are available in several different forms: dry, wet, semi-moist, and frozen (see page 100).

Feeding Frequency

If your little one is less than three months old, you should feed him four or five times a day—it's difficult, if not impossible, for puppies this age to consume adequate amounts of nutrients when fed less often. When he's three to five months old, decrease the number of feedings to three or four a day. (Don't forget to increase his total daily intake as he grows.) When your puppy is six months old, decrease the number of feedings to the adult schedule of two meals a day. If your little buddy is susceptible to hypoglycemia (see below), your veterinarian may recommend more frequent meals.

When your little Pom is 9 to 12 months old, he'll be ready to graduate to adult food. Make the change gradually, to avoid causing any digestive upsets. On the first day, replace 25 percent of his puppy food with the adult food. On the second day, give him equal portions of puppy food and adult food. On the third day, replace 75 percent of his puppy food with the adult food. On the fourth day, eliminate the puppy food completely.

Hypoglycemia

Hypoglycemia is a potentially life-threatening disorder that most commonly afflicts toy breed puppies less than four months of age. Factors that make toy breed puppies more susceptible to hypoglycemia include a large brain (a major user of glucose) relative to the size of the muscle mass and liver (areas where glucose is stored as glycogen), and high activity level. In some puppies, immaturity reduces the body's ability to process and store glucose.

The symptoms—trembling, lethargy, incoordination, and mental confusion—occur when the brain is deprived of glucose, its sole energy source. If not promptly treated, hypoglycemia can lead to seizures, unconsciousness, and death. Strenuous exercise, stressful situations (such as a trip to the veterinarian), and going too long without eating can all trigger hypoglycemia in a susceptible puppy.

If your Pom puppy develops signs of hypoglycemia, you'll need to take action immediately. Wrap him in a towel or blanket to keep him warm (shivering will make the hypoglycemia worse). If he's conscious, dribble a little corn syrup or honey into his mouth or give him a dab of high-calorie dietary supplement paste such as Nutri-Cal. Repeat at 10 minute intervals, if needed (if your puppy doesn't recover completely after three treatments, contact your veterinarian). Feed your youngster as soon as he's able to eat.

If the hypoglycemia makes your Pom lose consciousness, rub the syrup or paste on his gums and tongue (the glucose will be absorbed through these surfaces), but don't give him anything that he has to swallow. Immediately take him to your veterinarian or emergency clinic for further care.

Puppies that are susceptible to hypoglycemia need to eat high-quality, nutritionally balanced food four to five times a day (your veterinarian may recommend more feedings). Feeding healthful, high-calorie snacks in between meals may help stave off hypoglycemic episodes. As much as possible, reduce your Pom's exposure to circumstances that may trigger hypoglycemia, such as stressful situations or extended periods of strenuous exercise. Most puppies outgrow hypoglycemia by the time they're four months old; consult your veterinarian if the problem persists after this age.

Puppy-Proofing

Once you're all set up to provide the basics of food and shelter, you'll need to puppy-proof your home and yard (or at least the areas where your puppy will be). This won't be easy, because puppies have an uncanny knack for getting into all kinds of dangerous stuff.

The hazards fall into two very broad categories: things that are dangerous if your puppy eats or chews them (for example, toxic chemicals, poisonous plants, and electrical cords) and items or structures that can cause external injury (for example, broken glass, decks, and swimming pools).

The following defense strategies will help you protect your little friend:

- **Elimination:** Get rid of the hazard.
- **Substitution:** Replace dangerous products with safer ones. For example, use nontoxic white vinegar to clean bathroom faucets and surfaces. Use propylene glycol antifreeze, which is much less toxic (though not nontoxic) than ethylene glycol antifreeze.
- **Obstruction:** Make it impossible for your puppy to get to the hazard. Hide electrical cords behind furniture. Put dangerous items in locked cabinets (check out childproof locks at the hardware store); on high shelves; in puppy-proof storage containers; or in a closet, storeroom,

BE PREPARED! Puppy Hazards

Hazard	Result	Additional Information
Fabric and fiber goods	Digestive tract obstruction if swallowed.	—
Electrical cords	Electric shock if chewed; strangulation.	—
Ropes, cords, strings	Digestive tract obstruction or injury if swallowed.	A single strand of string or cord can cause serious digestive tract damage by cutting into the intestines as they contract around it.
Plants	Toxic reaction if chewed or ingested; mouth irritation, if chewed.	—
Solvents and other chemicals	Toxic reaction if ingested; local irritation after direct contact.	A nasty smell or taste won't always keep the puppy from ingesting the product.
Cleaning supplies	Toxic reaction if ingested; local irritation after direct contact.	Puppy may ingest the product despite its unappealing smell or taste.
Lawn and garden products	Toxic reaction if ingested or absorbed through skin; local irritation after direct contact.	Exposure may occur when a puppy walks where the product has been applied and then licks his feet.
Pesticides	Toxic reaction after ingestion or direct contact.	Rodent pesticides are often incorporated into edible baits, which may be attractive to puppies.
Medications (veterinary and human)	Toxic reaction after ingestion.	Especially dangerous: flavored medications such as pediatric preparations and heartworm preventives. A puppy can easily chew through child-proof containers.
Foods (see page 103)	Vomiting, diarrhea, and other toxic reactions after ingestion.	Safety for people doesn't always mean safety for puppies. Check with your veterinarian before feeding any type of "people food."
Toys, that can be swallowed, splintered, or that contain batteries.	Mouth injury, if chewed; digestive tract obstruction/injury, if swallowed; choking; toxic reaction (batteries).	—
Environmental or structural dangers	Various injuries (external and internal) from falling.	—

BE PREPARED! Puppy Hazards (continued)

Hazard	Result	Additional Information
Office supplies	External injury from direct contact; digestive tract obstruction/injury if swallowed; toxic reaction following ingestion; strangulation.	—
Sewing supplies	External injury from direct contact; digestive tract obstruction/injury if swallowed; choking; strangulation.	—
Fishing equipment	External injury from direct contact; digestive tract obstruction/injury if swallowed.	Residual "fishy" smell may be particularly enticing for puppies.
Christmas decorations	External injury if puppy breaks a glass ornament; digestive tract obstruction after ingestion of tinsel or garlands.	Most decorations are made of nontoxic materials. Poinsettias, which are mistakenly thought to be quite toxic, usually cause only minor mouth irritation.
Sharp objects	Various injuries (external and internal) following direct contact or ingestion.	—
Swimming pools	Drowning.	—

or attic. Barricades and fences are useful both inside and outside, but they must be strong enough and high enough to keep your puppy from getting through them or over them. When you can't supervise your puppy, put him in a crate, exercise pen, or a completely puppy-proofed area, such as a laundry room, bathroom, or outdoor dog pen.

• **Education:** Teach family members that everyone is responsible for the puppy's safety. Teach them to always close cabinets, doors, and gates, and not to leave hazardous items lying around where the puppy can get into them. Teach them which foods are "okay" and which are not (younger children may not understand this, so simply tell them that the puppy gets only puppy food, not "people food").

• **Stimulation:** Your baby Pom needs mental stimulation, physical activity, and human companionship. If you don't spend enough time with your puppy, he may turn to destructive (and potentially dangerous) activities in an effort to relieve his boredom and frustration.

• **Supervision:** This is your most important defense tactic—the one that can overcome the shortcomings of all the others. As with a small child, there's just no substitute for keeping your eye on that little one all the time.

The Pom Place

Set up your baby Pom's bed (his carrier or crate, lined with newspapers and soft towels or a blanket) in a quiet room or area away from the major traffic areas of the house. Choose a location that's close enough for you to keep track of him, but not so close that he'll be howling just outside your bedroom door at night. This will be his special spot, a cozy retreat where he can sleep and get away from the hustle and bustle of the household.

At night, you'll confine your puppy to his crate. This will keep him in bed, which will help him learn that he has his own place to sleep—and it's not with you. Nighttime confinement will also get your puppy used to being in his crate, which will pay off later on when you need to confine him for housetraining or travel.

Homecoming

Your baby Pom is bound to be a little nervous when you first bring him home, so take things slowly at first. It's all new to him and he's going to need some time to get used to everything.

First, show your newcomer his bed, as well as his food and water dishes (don't forget to put some food and water in his dishes). Then let him explore his surroundings at his own pace. He may stay right next to you or he may charge ahead to check out the territory. As much as possible, don't interfere during his exploration. You and your family can watch, of course, but it's

better to let your newcomer go at his own pace. Let him decide when to approach the family members, not the other way around. Be particularly careful about allowing young children to handle him and play with him. Puppies are so much fun that it's hard for children (and some adults) to stop playing with them, even when the puppy is obviously exhausted. If you have other dogs and cats, remove them from the puppy's area for the time being. You'll have plenty of time to introduce them later (remember, your puppy might not even know what a cat is!).

Nighty-Night

Don't be surprised if your puppy has a little trouble sleeping the first night. After all, he's in a strange new place, away from his mom and littermates. He's probably never slept by himself. Does this mean you should let him sleep with you or maybe just put his bed in your bedroom? Not unless you want to have him sleep with you forever. The quickest way to get him used to sleeping where he belongs—in his own bed in his own special spot—is to make him do it from the very beginning. He also needs to learn that he won't always be able to be with you. If he doesn't learn that lesson early, future separations (for example, if you go on a trip without him) could be extremely traumatic for him.

At bedtime, after you've given your baby Pom a snack and taken him outside for a potty break, take him to his special spot, fluff up his bed a bit, and put him in his crate. Then tell him good night, close the crate door, and leave. Don't check on him unless you hear some sort of terrible noise (beyond puppy fussing), such as the crate falling over. It will be hard to stay away, especially if your little one cries, but if you respond to his cries, he'll learn that all he has to do is cry loud enough and you'll come to him. If you can't resist checking on him, wait until he stops fussing—if only briefly—and then go to him, praising him for being quiet. Check him quickly and then leave.

If it makes you feel better, you can use the alarm clock trick—wrap an old-fashioned ticking alarm clock in a towel and put it in his bed. Supposedly, the ticking will remind your puppy of his mother's heartbeat and soothe him to sleep. Unfortunately, this never seems to work as well as it's supposed to! You can also try playing soft music, which may comfort him. If you use this tactic, be sure to place the audio equipment and cords, if any, where your little friend can't reach them.

Setting Limits

Decide early where you will allow your Pom in the house. Will he have the run of the entire house or will there be certain areas that are off-limits? If you decide to restrict your puppy's access to some areas, you need to be firm and consistent about enforcing the limits. At first, restrict his access by closing doors or putting up removable gates or barriers. If you can't do that, you'll need to keep a careful watch for trespassing. When your little buddy wanders into a restricted area, pick him up, repri-mand him mildly, and put him back in the per-mitted area. Try to catch him just as he is about to cross the boundary—when teaching a lesson, it's always better to catch the error right before it happens than after the fact. Don't ever give in and let him stay in an off-limits area "just this once." After a while, your youngster will learn that there are certain areas of the house where he's not allowed. It will be a whole lot easier to keep him in his permitted area if you're there too.

In addition to limiting your puppy's access to certain areas of the house, you may want to teach him to stay off the fur-niture. First decide what you will and will not permit. It'll be less confusing for your little one if you make all furniture, rather than just some furniture, off-limits. When your little one violates the rules, pick him up, reprimand him in a firm tone of voice, and place him on the floor. Be consistent—don't be tempted to bend the rules. Repeat this procedure as many times as necessary. Your Pom will soon learn that his proper place is on the floor, not the furniture. Finally, remember to occasionally get down on the floor to play with your puppy so he won't have to climb on the furniture to get your attention.

Housetraining

It's easy to understand why the necessity of housetraining makes prospective dog owners think twice before adopting a puppy: A dog that's not reliably housetrained isn't much fun to have in the house, yet few owners want to banish their companion to a life outdoors. Add the inevitable questions about housetraining—how to do it, when to do it—and you have a situation that almost always creates tension for both the dog owner and the dog.

Housetraining doesn't have to be like that. It really isn't much different from teaching your youngster to sit or lie down. As with any training, it's going to take time for him to learn what he needs to do.

Start housetraining your puppy when he's four to six months old. He'll have better control and it will be easier for him to understand what you want him to do. It's all right, of course, to take a younger puppy outside to eliminate. Just don't expect too much too soon. Ignore his mistakes, but be sure to praise him when he does the right thing.

The direct method of housetraining, which involves taking the puppy outside to relieve himself, is convenient for owners who have easy access to outdoors. It works best if the owner spends a lot of time at home. Owners who live in apartments or who are frequently away from home may have more success with the second method of housetraining, which uses paper training as an intermediate step toward the goal of outside elimination.

Helpful Hints

Housetraining Tips

When housetraining, make it easy for your puppy to choose the correct behavior.

Be considerate: Don't confine him in his crate for too long (no more hours than he is months old, up to six hours maximum at any age).

Use his instincts: Confine him in a crate or small room to take advantage of his basic canine desire to keep the den or nest clean.

Accompany him: When your Pom needs to relieve himself, don't just put him outside; take him to the place where he's gone before (or where you want him to) and praise him when he does it again.

Schedule his breaks: Puppies usually need to eliminate after eating, waking up, and playing. Get in the habit of taking him out at those times.

Don't punish: If your puppy has an accident, reprimand him mildly, but only if you catch him in the act. Don't reprimand him at all if you discover a pile or puddle after the fact. He won't associate your correction with the act.

Direct Housetraining

For direct housetraining, you'll need to get your puppy a crate or carrier, if you don't already have one. It should be roomy enough that he can turn around in it, but not so large that he can use one end as a bathroom and "escape" to the other end. Line the crate with newspapers and some soft towels or a blanket for a bed. Try to find a crate that has a built-in holder for a water bowl or bottle, so your little one can have water while he's confined (he'll eat his meals outside the crate). It's important to make this indoor doghouse as comfortable as possible, because you want your puppy to enjoy his time there.

When your puppy needs to relieve himself—after eating, after naps, or any other time he shows signs of needing to go out—take him outside to his designated "potty spot." When you return to the house, put your youngster back in his crate. It's okay to keep him in a restricted space such as the kitchen, as long as you can watch him closely. If your puppy relieves himself inside, reprimand him mildly (if you see him do it), then take him outside to his spot. He'll soon learn that it's inappropriate (and unpleasant, if he's confined to his crate) to eliminate in the house.

Direct housetraining using a crate or carrier is fast and efficient. The necessary confinement and supervision requires some effort, but it's definitely easier than struggling with housetraining for months or even years.

Paper-Training

For paper-training, select a small, tile-floored room, such as a bathroom or laundry room (puppy-proofed, of course), where you can confine your puppy. If you don't want to use a room, you can set up an exercise pen in a suitable location. You'll want your puppy to be comfortable, so put his crate or carrier (with the door open) in the room or exercise pen, along with water, food, and a few puppy-safe toys. Cover the entire floor with several layers of newspapers and confine your Pom in the room. When he uses the papers, clean up the soiled papers and replace them.

Continue like this for a day or two, then leave one corner of the room or pen bare. He'll probably continue to use the papers or maybe even the same general area where he's gone before. If he slips up and eliminates on the unpapered floor, don't reprimand him unless you catch him in the act. Even then, simply scold him mildly and put him on the papers. When he hits the papers every time, gradually take them up until the papered area is only a two-foot (60 cm) square. Let him use that area until you start taking him outside to relieve himself. At first, you'll have to take him outside frequently. Once he learns that outside is the appropriate place for elimination, you can stop using the papers.

ID Required

Even though your Pom is just a youngster, it's never too soon to think about some sort of identification for him, which he should wear at all times. Even if he's always in a fenced yard or on a leash, there's always a chance he could escape.

Tags Your Pom's identification doesn't have to be elaborate. It could be as simple as your phone number scratched on the metal plate of his collar. Better yet, you could have a special identification tag made that lists your name, address, and phone number. Tags are better than no identification at all, but because they're attached to the dog's collar, they can be easily lost or removed. If the collar comes off, so does the identification. Because of this, a tag won't protect your Pom from being stolen.

Tattooing A more permanent method of identification is tattooing, which can be done by a veterinarian. Unfortunately, your Pom's small size will limit the amount of information his tattoo can contain. Tattooing offers more security against theft than collars and tags, but it doesn't provide absolute protection because tattoos can fade and alteration is possible.

Microchipping The implantation of a data chip under the skin on the back of the neck is the most sophisticated and theft-proof means of identification. The microchip, which is about the size of a grain of rice, contains an identification number that can be read with a special scanner. The identification number, along with owner identification, is registered in a database maintained by the microchip manufacturer or other lost dog program, such as the AKC Companion Animal Recovery Program. Someone who finds a lost dog can't tell if it's been microchipped (and wouldn't be able to access the information if they did know), but many animal shelters and veterinary clinics have microchip scanners. The average person can't remove or alter a microchip.

The Great Outdoors

Your Pom puppy will undoubtedly enjoy being outdoors, but you can't just shove him out the door. At first, you'll need to go with him (to keep him company and make sure he's safe). When he's about four months old, he can go outside by himself for playtime, but continue to accompany him for housetraining trips. Keep his outdoor excursions short at first—15 minutes or so—and gradually lengthen them until he's staying out for up to two hours at a time.

Regardless of whether you're with him or not, your baby Pom needs a safe, comfortable place to play and relax. His space should be puppy-proofed and have shade, shelter, and comfy lounging spots. Don't forget that he'll need water whenever he's outside for more than a few minutes. Giving him a little snack will help him enjoy his outdoor playtime even more.

The surface of your puppy's play place can be either grass or concrete, but not bare dirt. Grass is cooler and more comfortable on the paws, but concrete surfaces are easier to clean and less likely to harbor fleas, ticks, and internal

FYI: Invisible Fences

Invisible fences operate on radio waves. The dog wears a special collar that picks up a signal emitted from a wire that has been buried around the yard's perimeter. When the dog approaches the perimeter, the fence emits a high-frequency warning sound. If the dog stops, nothing happens. If he continues toward the perimeter, the collar emits a brief shock that's uncomfortable but not painful. The dog quickly learns to turn away when he hears the warning signal.

Invisible fences have several disadvantages:

- They're effective only if all of the components are working correctly and the dog is wearing the collar. If any component fails or your Pom slips out of the collar, there's nothing to keep him in the yard.
- An invisible fence won't keep other dogs out of your yard, which means that your Pom will be unprotected against dogs that are aggressive, sick, or apt to cause other problems.
- If your pal happens to cross the fence line in a moment of excitement (for example, chasing a squirrel), he won't want to return to the yard because he'll get shocked.

parasites. If the play area has a hard surface, be sure to provide some soft bedding so your youngster can lounge around (or nap) in comfort.

Your Pom play space needs to be adequately fenced. Your little buddy won't need a huge fence, even when he's all grown up; 2½ feet (75 cm) high should be sufficient. A wooden fence must have slats that are close enough together that your puppy won't be able to slip out between them. Using chain link or woven wire will solve this problem and let your puppy watch all the interesting things going on outside the yard. If your yard is unfenced, very large, or difficult to puppy-proof, you can use an exercise pen for your

Pom's enclosure. Exercise pens are convenient because they're portable and easy to set up, which allows you to move your little buddy's play space to different spots in your yard whenever you want.

Your youngster will need a doghouse if he's going to be outside for more than a potty break. Place the house in a shady, sheltered area of your yard (or your pal's enclosure). If possible, position it with the door facing south to protect your friend from cold north winds in the winter and allow southern breezes to enter the house in the summer.

Walking with your Pom is a good way to share some "together" time while you both get a little exercise. For your pal's safety, you'll need to always keep him on a leash during your walks, but don't just slap a collar and leash on him and go; give him a little time to get used to them first (see the chapter on Training and Activities for how to do this). Take your first walks inside, and then go outside and walk in your yard. When your puppy is comfortable walking in the yard, you can venture into the "outside world," *as long as he's up-to-date on his vaccinations and at least 16 weeks old (the age when he's likely to be fully protected by those vaccinations).* If he gets nervous, go back to walking in your yard for a while before trying again.

The Weather Report

If your Pom will eventually spend more than just a few minutes outside, you'll need to make sure he's comfortable when the weather is less than perfect. In cold weather, bed his house with thick blankets, cedar shaving–filled pads, or an electric heating mat designed for outdoor use. Straw also makes a soft, warm bed as long as you use enough, but be forewarned: You'll spend a lot of time brushing it out of your little pal's coat. Baled straw placed around the house also provides good insulation. Don't forget that your Pom will also need water even when it's cold outside. Provide fresh water several times a day or use a heat lamp or heated water bowl to keep it from freezing.

In the summertime, you'll have just the opposite problem—how to keep your pal cool. He'll tolerate hot weather better if he's gradually gotten acclimated to it and has ample shade and water, but you'll still need to watch carefully to make sure he doesn't get overheated. That fluffy Pom coat is great in the winter, but it can make it hard for your guy to stay cool when the temperatures soar. Because of this, don't leave him outside without supervision on a hot summer day; instead, use barriers or an exercise pen to set up an indoor play place.

CAUTION

Hot Tip

In hot weather, you may be able to let your Pom enjoy the great outdoors in the mornings or evenings when the temperatures are relatively mild, but you'll still need to watch him carefully for signs of overheating. Be sure to provide adequate shade and water whenever you let your Pom outdoors without direct supervision.

10 Questions About Puppy Health Care

1 What will happen at my puppy's first visit to the veterinarian? First, your veterinarian will ask about your Pom's vaccinations, deworming, illnesses or injuries, and diet. Next, he or she will examine your puppy, check a stool sample for intestinal parasites, if possible, and give any necessary vaccinations. Finally, your veterinarian will make recommendations and answer your questions about future vaccinations, deworming, heartworm prevention, spaying/neutering, and other health issues.

2 What vaccinations does my puppy need? Your puppy, like all dogs, needs core vaccinations against rabies, distemper, infectious hepatitis, and parvovirus. Noncore vaccinations against less serious diseases, such as leptospirosis and kennel cough, are recommended only for high-risk dogs and puppies—for example, those that attend shows. Your veterinarian can tell you which vaccinations your puppy needs.

Your puppy needs at least one distemper/hepatitis/parvovirus vaccination by the time he's six to eight weeks old, with additional vaccinations every three to four weeks until he's at least 16 weeks of age (18 to 20 weeks for parvovirus). He should receive his first rabies vaccination at 16 weeks of age, with a booster when he's one year old.

3 How can I keep my puppy healthy? The most serious threats to your puppy's health are diseases spread by other dogs. Vaccination is the best protection, but keep him away from sick and unvaccinated dogs too, especially if he hasn't had all of his vaccinations. Other ways to keep your little one healthy: control internal parasites (such as roundworms, hookworms, and heartworms) and external parasites (such as fleas and ticks); keep him in a fenced yard or on a leash when he's outside; and feed him a completely balanced puppy food.

4 Why is it important to spay or neuter a puppy? Spaying or neutering ensures that the puppy, when grown, will never contribute to the huge population of unwanted dogs, but there are other benefits too. Surgical neutering of males often decreases roaming and fighting, and reduces or eliminates some prostate and testicular diseases. A spayed female won't come into heat, so there's no bloody discharge and the canine suitors it attracts. Spaying also eliminates uterine infections and, in some cases, decreases the incidence of mammary cancer.

5 When is the best time to have a puppy spayed or neutered? Puppies can be spayed or surgically neutered when they're as young as eight weeks of age, but many veterinarians recommend waiting until four to six months. Chemical neutering is performed only on puppies between the ages of three and ten months. Your veterinarian can advise you about the best time to have your puppy spayed or neutered.

6 **How can I tell if my puppy has worms?** You can't always tell, because most worms (intestinal parasites) can't be seen with the naked eye and symptoms often don't occur until the puppy becomes heavily parasitized. Symptoms of severe roundworm infection include abdominal distension, intestinal blockage, diarrhea, dull hair coat, and stunted growth. Heavy hookworm infections can cause anemia, weakness, diarrhea (possibly tarry or bloody), and weight loss. Your veterinarian can determine if your puppy has intestinal parasites by examining a stool sample under a microscope.

7 **What are heartworms?** Heartworms are spread by mosquitoes. The female mosquito ingests microfilariae (immature heartworms) when she feeds on an infected dog. The microfilariae develop in the mosquito, who introduces them into another dog while feeding. The larval heartworms eventually lodge in the arteries of the lungs, where they develop into adults and reproduce. In heavy infections, the heartworms may also occur in the large vessels between the heart and the lungs, and even in the heart itself. Heavy infections can cause coughing, shortness of breath, and exercise intolerance. Untreated heartworm infection can lead to heart failure and death.

8 **How can I keep my puppy from getting heartworms?** You can prevent heartworms by giving your puppy medication (usually a monthly pill, chewable tablet, or spot-on) throughout the mosquito season. Some preventives can be given to puppies as young as four weeks of age. If your puppy is older than six months, your veterinarian can also inject a preventive that lasts for six months.

Puppies that are less than six months old when started on preventive should be tested for heartworms six to twelve months later. Older puppies should be tested before starting the preventive.

9 **How can I tell if my puppy has fleas or ticks?** You probably won't have trouble seeing ticks on your puppy, but fleas are harder to spot. Check his neck, abdomen, and tail base—places where fleas like to hang out. If you don't see the critters, you may find their excrement—reddish-brown stuff that looks like dirt.

10 **How can I get rid of my puppy's fleas and ticks?** Many flea control products also control ticks, but the duration of effect may be shorter. Thoroughly vacuuming your home will reduce the flea population by eliminating some of the eggs, larvae, and excrement. Washing your puppy's bedding will also help. If the fleas persist in your home, apply a household insecticide.

If your Pom spends time in your yard, you'll need to spray it for fleas and ticks. For fleas, you'll probably need to treat only your pal's favorite spots and paths, but if you're fighting ticks you may need to spray the entire yard. Other tick-fighting tactics include mowing your lawn, removing overgrown brush, and fencing your yard to keep tick-bearing wild animals (such as deer) out.

Chapter Five

Living with
a Pomeranian

You and your Pomeranian have made it through the first year; your best friend has officially achieved adult status. Although you undoubtedly caught glimpses of the "Pom-to-be" when he was a puppy, now you'll actually get to meet that dog, as you and your buddy forge a mature and lasting friendship.

Your Adult Pom

It's hard to say what the "average" adult Pomeranian is like, because every Pomeranian is unique, a little bit different from all the others. Like all of us, each one has good points and each one has some that aren't so good. Then too, you have to consider that aging is a transition for dogs, just as it is for people, with considerable overlap between the stages. Generally speaking, however, your adult Pom is likely to be:

- **Independent:** As your Pom gets older and learns more about his family and surroundings, he'll naturally become more independent, but he'll still need your companionship.
- **Self-Confident:** This may prompt him to try to assert his dominance over other dogs and possibly humans. As much as possible, you should let the dogs work out their own differences, but you may have to intervene if your little friend challenges a much larger dog. Displays of dominance toward humans should not be tolerated.
- **More Focused:** Your Pom's attention span will be longer, which means he'll learn things more quickly. Then again, it also means that he'll be less easily distracted and more persistent when it comes to doing things his own way.
- **Energetic:** Even though he's no longer a puppy, your pal will still have a lot of energy. It's just part of being a Pom.
- **Resilient:** Greater stamina means he'll be able to stay active for longer periods of time. He'll still enjoy naps, but he just won't need as many.

- **Less Playful:** This is a definite "maybe" that depends on your Pom's basic personality. Some of these little live wires keep their playful attitude throughout adulthood.
- **Less Likely to Chew:** Most dogs like to chew, even when they're adults. Your adult Pom may be less likely to chew the wrong things, but don't count on it: Keep track of what he's got his teeth around.
- **Housetrained:** Ideally your buddy is housetrained. If he's not, getting him there may be difficult, but it won't be impossible, even if he's an older adult. Be persistent.

Caring for Your Adult Pom

Raising a puppy takes a lot of time and effort. Once your Pom reaches adulthood, you might feel like you can finally catch your breath and relax a little bit. After all, the hard part's done, right?

Not exactly. Even though your pal is all grown up (at least physically) and way more self-sufficient than he was as a puppy, he still needs a lot of care that only you can give him. It's particularly important that you continue to provide regular health care, good nutrition, exercise, social structure, mental stimulation, and lots of social opportunities.

Regular Health and Dental Care He won't need vaccinations as frequently as he did when he was a puppy, but he'll still need them. Taking care of his teeth will increase the likelihood that he'll keep those teeth throughout adulthood and his senior years.

Good Nutrition Feed him a completely balanced dog food, which will give him all the nutrients he needs. Resist the urge to overindulge him with table food or too many between-meal treats. He doesn't need as many calories now, so extra goodies can mean extra pounds.

Exercise As a puppy, your Pom got plenty of exercise just playing and running around. Chances are he'll be an active adult too, but if he isn't, you'll need to make sure he gets some vigorous exercise every day.

Social Structure Your buddy may be a full-grown, confident adult dog, but you're still the leader of the pack. Don't be afraid to take charge; you'll both be happier.

Helpful Hints

Best Friends Forever

You are the center of your Pom's universe, so don't deprive him of your companionship and make him spend most of his time alone. Share your life with him—you'll both be better for it.

Mental Stimulation Keep your Pom mentally sharp with training, games, and other activities. You'll both have fun, and working together will strengthen your friendship. It will also keep your pal from getting bored, which can lead to behavior problems such as chewing and excessive barking.

Social Interactions Dogs are social creatures. Give your Pom plenty of opportunities to socialize with other dogs and people.

Behavior Problems

As your Pom gets older, the chances of him developing behavior problems increase, for a lot of reasons. Perhaps you've been a little too lenient; perhaps he's gotten more persistent about getting his own way. Whatever the reason, it doesn't mean you have to resign yourself to living with behavior problems. With a little effort (or maybe more than a little in some cases), you can help your Pom break those bad habits.

Separation Anxiety

If your Pom had his way, he'd spend every minute of every day with you. Much as you'd enjoy that too, real life intervenes on a regular basis, forcing you to juggle family, work, school, and other responsibilities. Your pal doesn't understand this, so when you leave the house to go to work or run an errand, he only knows that you've left—without him.

Many dogs tolerate spending some of their time alone, especially if it's only for a few hours and they have toys, food, or other activities (for example, patrolling the yard) to keep them occupied. Some dogs, however, develop separation anxiety, becoming distressed and agitated when their owners leave, or even get ready to leave.

The main symptoms of separation anxiety occur once the owner has left and include destructive behavior (chewing, scratching), vocalization (whining, barking, howling), pacing, house-soiling, drooling, and self-mutilation (excessive licking or chewing).

If your Pom has separation anxiety, you can try several tactics to reduce or eliminate it. First, make sure your pal has toys and food to keep him busy while you're gone. Some dogs do better if they stay outside, but this won't work if the weather doesn't cooperate.

Next, you'll need to desensitize him to your departures. He's figured out that you always do certain things before you leave the house—brush your hair, get your coat, find the car keys, and so on. When he sees you doing those things, he gets upset because he knows you're going to leave. To desensitize him to these cues, act like you're getting ready to go somewhere, but don't leave; simply sit down and watch television or read a book.

When your buddy calmly accepts your getting-ready routine, leave the house every once in a while for a very brief time (five minutes is plenty). Give your Pom a verbal signal such as *"See you later!"* to reassure him that you'll return. Use this signal every time you leave. You can also use a physical signal such as giving him a special toy (that he doesn't get to play with any other time). When you return, greet him matter-of-factly, then ignore him for a few minutes. Gradually increase the length of time that you're gone, always giving him the signal before you leave and always ignoring him for a short time after you return. Your goal is to teach him that it's no big deal when you leave or return—and that you'll always return.

If, despite your best efforts, your Pom continues to be anxious about your comings and goings, ask your veterinarian about medication, such as clomipramine (Clomicalm), which was developed specifically to treat separation anxiety. Some experts recommend using DAP (Dog Appeasing Pheromone), a synthetic compound that mimics naturally occurring pheromones secreted by a lactating female. This product, which is available in collar, spray, and diffusible aerosol forms, is undetectable to humans, but induces feelings of reassurance and well-being in dogs.

Excessive Barking

A dog that barks all the time can drive even the most devoted dog lover crazy, even if that dog lover happens to be the dog's owner. It's not difficult to imagine how the neighbors feel about it.

If your Pom barks because he's defending his territory when he's out in the yard, you may have let him outside at a different time or moved him to an area where he can't see every person that walks by. If he's inside and barks when someone comes to the door, after a few barks say, *"Fluffy, that's enough!"* and make him sit down (put a leash on him if necessary). Repeat this lesson until he learns that it's okay to alert you, but not okay to keep barking.

If your Pom barks because he's bored, anxious, or lonely, correcting the root cause should fix the problem. Spend more time with him—training, playing, or just being together. Don't isolate him away from you and your

FYI: Why Is He Barking?

Your Pom has a good reason for barking, at least to his way of thinking:

- He's defending his territory.
- He's bored.
- He's anxious.
- He's lonely.
- He's excited.

family. Don't leave him by himself for so long or so often. If you must leave him for hours each day (for example, when you go to work), consider recruiting a neighbor or hiring a pet sitter to stop by and play with him while you're gone. Taking him to doggie day care is another option that may be available, depending on where you live.

If your buddy barks simply because he's excited, don't yell at him—he'll just think you're barking right along with him. Instead, wait until he's quiet, even for just a moment, then praise him and give him a treat. At first, you may have to distract him to get him to stop barking (try tossing a coin-filled can in his direction) long enough to reward him. Gradually increase the length of time your pal has to wait before he gets the reward. Next, add a cue word such as *"Shh!"* Eventually he'll figure out that he'll get a treat if he's quiet after you give him the cue.

Breed Truths

What's Yours Is Yours

From a nutritional standpoint, it's okay to feed your Pom a little table food. From a behavior standpoint, it's not a good idea. If you never give your buddy table food, he'll be less likely to think that your food is his food, which may keep him from taking up begging as his favorite hobby.

Begging

It's hard to resist that cute little guy in the fancy fur coat when he gazes lovingly up at you and asks for just a tiny morsel of your dinner. So you give in, just this once, only to discover that "once" wasn't what he had in mind at all. You've just helped your Pom start his begging career.

It's easier to prevent begging (just say no—every time, without exceptions), but if your pal is already a confirmed beggar, here's how to put a stop to it for good:

- Feed him when you eat, but in another room.
- Ignore him when he begs, no matter where you are or what he's begging for (usually food, but some dogs beg for attention). Realize that

HOME BASICS
Settle!

Another way to calm down an excited dog is by teaching him to settle. Teaching Fluffy to settle will be easier if he's already learned the *down* command. While he's in the *down* position, gently lay him on his side and say, *"Fluffy, settle!"* As you hold him in that position, repeat the command, but don't sweet-talk him. Praise him when he relaxes, if only for a few seconds. Release your pal before he starts to struggle, accompanying your release with *"Okay."* You may have to be satisfied with just a few seconds of settling at first, then gradually work up to longer periods. Always praise your Pom when he settles for any length of time.

Continue working until your friend will settle on his own. At first, give the command only when he's already calm (it's easier if he's already lying down too). Keep these initial solo runs short—no longer than a minute. Gradually increase the amount of time and finally, ask your Pom to settle during more stressful situations. Be patient: It will take some time for your buddy to figure out what *"Settle"* means and to understand that you don't have to hold him in position.

Note: Before you try to teach this command, assess your Pom's personality; if you think he may become defensive and try to bite you during training sessions, *do not* try to teach him to settle without seeking the advice or assistance of an experienced trainer.

he'll probably increase his efforts dramatically as you continue to ignore him, before finally giving up.
- Instruct family members and guests that they are not to give in to begging behavior—not even once.
- If necessary, have your Pom stay in another room while you eat. Use the *go lie down* command if he knows it. If he won't stay away, confine him in the room or in a crate, but make sure he's got something to keep him occupied while he's confined.
- Be persistent. He's hoping you'll eventually give in, and he's willing to wait.

Chewing
Chewing is one of those behaviors that's both normal (physiological) and abnormal (psychological). Either way, it can cause problems.

Puppies chew for physiological reasons during teething and as they investigate their surroundings by putting everything in their mouths. These little ones don't need correction, but they do need plenty of safe chew toys, so they don't decide to do their teething on the leg of your best antique chair. During this stage, it's important to make sure that your house and yard are thoroughly puppy-proofed.

Adult dogs often chew for psychological reasons, usually because they're bored, anxious, or lonely. If this sounds like your Pom, you need to address the basic problem. Spend as much time with your buddy as possible. If you're gone for most of the day, take your pal for a walk or jog when you get home and spend the evening together; get up a little earlier in the morning so you can have a little time together before you go to work. Enroll in an obedience class and schedule daily training sessions. These measures will probably reduce your pal's chewing, but just for good measure, keep him in a dog-safe area and make sure he has suitable toys in case he decides to do a little chewing.

Jumping Up

"Get down!" is a phrase dogs hear a lot—and ignore a lot, while they continue to jump up on their owners, household guests, and total strangers.

When your Pom jumps up on you, he's probably just trying to say, "Hi there! I'm so glad to see you!" You're not down on his level, so your buddy bounces as high as he can, ambitiously trying to greet you in canine nose-to-nose fashion.

Jumping up isn't always a friendly behavior, however; some dogs jump up to assert their dominance. In the canine world, physical elevation and initiation of physical interaction are strong dominance signals. Adult dogs jump up to display their dominance more frequently than puppies, often targeting children, strangers, or anyone that is perceived as subordinate or easily dominated.

Even though jumping up is normal canine behavior, you don't have to tolerate it. You can teach your buddy to control his natural instincts and replace jumping up with behavior that's more appropriate for human-dog interactions.

Before you can teach your Pom not to jump up, you'll need to teach him to sit and stay (the *sit-stay*) on command. This

serves several purposes. First, the *sit-stay* is the behavior that will replace jumping up. Second, every time your Pom obeys the *sit-stay* command, he's reminded of your dominant status. Finally, your pal won't be able to jump up if his bottom is firmly planted on the floor!

Your Pom must learn the *sit-stay* so thoroughly that he immediately responds to your command with a full *sit* and stays in that position until you say it's okay to move. If he won't do this every time you ask for it, work on it some more, before you try to teach him not to jump up.

Once your Pom sits and stays reliably whenever you tell him to, teach him to substitute that behavior for jumping up. You're going to set up a situation that brings out his inclination to jump up, such as walking in the front door, so be prepared. Wear old clothes that you don't mind getting dirty or torn. If you're going to use treats as a reward, put some in your pocket. Make sure your Pom is wearing his collar.

Next, leave your pal and briefly go outside or to another part of your house. When you return, be ready to act fast. When your Pom approaches you, don't say anything until he's about 5 to 6 feet (1.5–1.8 m) away from you, then give him the *sit-stay* command. This lets him know what you want him to do before he starts jumping up. When your buddy sits and stays, reward him immediately (with praise and a treat, if you're using them), and then greet him. If he doesn't obey you, take him by the collar and place him in a sitting position as you repeat the command, then reward and greet him. If you use this procedure every time your Pom comes to you, he'll eventually learn to politely sit and wait for your greeting. You'll need a little patience; it may take two weeks or even longer before he understands what you want him to do.

The method outlined above works well for most dogs, but if your Pom continues to jump up, you'll need to try another tactic. Set up the situation as before, giving the *sit-stay* command when your buddy approaches you. When he jumps up, grab his front paws, look directly at him, and say *"Ah-ah-ah!"* as you continue to hold his paws. (Saying *"Ah-ah-ah!"* is a non-harsh way of letting him know that he's making a mistake.) After a few seconds, he'll probably start to struggle and try to get away. Continue to hang on to his paws, without speaking, until he stops struggling. When this happens, release his paws and tell him to sit, placing him in position if necessary. Immediately reward him. Keep working like this until your Pom figures out that sitting is much more comfortable than jumping up.

You can also use the *sit-stay* method to teach your buddy not to jump up on guests and other non-family members, but you'll need the help of a friend. First, put a leash on your dog and a few treats in your pocket, if you're going to use them. Next, have your friend go outside, wait a few minutes, then ring the doorbell. Tell your Pom to sit and stay, then open the door and greet your friend, who should ignore your dog. If your Pom charges toward your friend, grab the leash and repeat the *sit-stay* command. If necessary, place him in the sitting position and hold him there. Once your dog sits, your friend can greet him in a cheerful but not exuberant manner. After the greeting, you (not your friend) should reward your dog for his polite behavior. Continue to work until your Pom learns that he'll be greeted only when he's sitting down. It may take awhile for him to figure this out.

Recruit other friends (adults and children) to help you get your dog used to being greeted by lots of different people. Don't just practice at home; make him sit for a greeting when you meet others while you're out walking. Organized classes are also good places to practice. Look for Canine Good Citizen classes, which spend a lot of time on proper greeting behavior. (The American Kennel Club awards the Canine Good Citizen Award to any dog, regardless of breed, that satisfactorily completes a test of basic manners. See the Training and Activities chapter for more information.)

Aggressive Behavior

Dogs bite for a lot of reasons. Puppies often bite when they play; older dogs sometimes do too. Some dogs bite when they're frightened. Still others bite because they're challenging your authority or protecting their territory, possessions, or people.

Playful Biting

Playful biting is normal behavior for a puppy, but that doesn't mean you have to tolerate it. Those needle-sharp baby teeth really hurt, even if it is just a playful bite. Some older dogs also engage in playful biting, especially if they've been encouraged to "rough-house" in the past. If you're

Helpful Hints

The Play's the Thing

When you're playing with your Pom, avoid games that involve chasing and/or biting. Don't play tug-of-war or other "fighting" games. It's okay to play ball and other retrieval games, if you don't let them turn into tug-of-war.

playing with your Pom and he bites you, even if it's an accident, immediately stop playing and say firmly, *"No bite!"* or *"No teeth!"* (Always use the same phrase.) Then completely ignore your dog for five to ten minutes. When you start playing again, choose a game that won't tempt your buddy to use his teeth. Going for a walk or working on obedience commands are good choices.

Fearful Biting (Fear Aggression)

Fearful biting occurs when the dog feels threatened and wants to escape, but can't. It's the classic fight-or-flight response: Since the dog can't flee, his only choice is to fight, so he defends himself by biting. This often occurs when a nervous, fearful dog is forced to submit to a stranger petting him.

He tries to convey his apprehension in the only way he knows how—by body language—but his signals are ignored. Unable to get away, he snaps at the approaching hand.

If your Pom is fear aggressive, helping him overcome his fears will make him less likely to bite. This can be accomplished only with slow, patient exposure to a wide variety of situations and people. Taking the following precautions can make this process easier for everyone involved:

- Don't put your Pom in situations that could make him afraid.
- If he acts inappropriately, don't punish him. That will only make things worse because he'll view it as a confirmation of his fears.
- When your friend is in a fear-inducing situation, don't corner him, reach for him, or otherwise force him to face his fears. Doing so will increase the likelihood that he will bite, which can lead to further fear aggression. Instead, call him to you and distract him by having him do an obedience task or trick for a reward.
- If he's misbehaving, don't reassure him or pet him. If you do, you'll send the message that he's acting appropriately, which he isn't.

Aggressive Biting

Aggressive biting occurs during possessive behavior, such as when the dog guards territory or belongings. It's also seen during displays of dominance, such as when the dog challenges authority.

Breed Truths

Dining Alone

To avoid triggering your Pom's food aggression, feed him in a quiet area that's away from the household hustle and bustle. Leave him alone while he eats and don't let other family members disturb him either. If necessary, confine him in his crate for his meals.

Possessive behavior is easy to understand: Your Pom, like all dogs, is hardwired to protect what he perceives as his stuff, whether it's his territory (your house and yard), food, or favorite toy. That doesn't mean it's okay for him to protect his possessions with his teeth, but at least you can figure out why he gets grumpy if he thinks you're going to take his food away.

Treating possessive behavior boils down to two basic tasks: Eliminate encounters and reward appropriate behavior. For instance, if your Pom is overly protective of his food, don't take it away from him in an effort to "get him used to it." That will just convince him that he's right to protect it. If you (or any other family member) must get near his food dish, teach him that he'll get a reward for politely tolerating it. Do this by dropping treats into his dish (or near it at first, if he acts threatened). Make sure the treat is one of his favorites. If, for some reason, you must take his food away, simultaneously replace it with a dish of tastier food.

Dominance-Related Aggression

Dominance-related aggression is the most dangerous type of aggression—and the most difficult to resolve. It's not hard to understand why it occurs: Power struggles are part of everyday life in the canine world, where the goal is to become the top dog in the pack, whether it's a pack of dogs, people, or something in between. Most domesticated dogs accept the leadership of their humans without question, at least most of the time. Some dogs are always looking for ways to climb the social ladder.

If your Pom has become one of these social climbers and repeatedly challenges your authority, you'll need to take some immediate steps to get back in charge.

Avoid Confrontations This doesn't mean backing down from a challenge; rather, it means using your head to avoid challenges in the first place. For example, if your Pom growls or snaps at you when you try to get him off his favorite chair, don't let him get up there in the first place (if necessary, rearrange the furniture or use gates or barriers).

Enroll in Obedience Class Obedience work can serve as a foundation for regaining and maintaining your authority. Every time you give a command and your dog obeys, you're reinforcing to him that you're in control. It doesn't have to be anything complicated: Just having him sit on command is enough. You can use this tactic whenever your pal needs a reminder about who's in charge. Obedience work also keeps his mind occupied, which means he won't be thinking of ways to take over.

Exercise Daily Making sure your Pom gets plenty of vigorous exercise every day will help him use up some of his extra energy. Ideally, he'll be too tired to challenge you. Another benefit: If you choose the activity, it's just another way to show him that you're the boss.

Think Like a Dog In a canine pack, the alpha member remains aloof and decides when or if interactions with other members will occur. Subordinate members try to please the alpha, not the other way around. If your Pom tries to take control, ignore him. Withhold everything (talking, petting, even food) unless he obeys a command. This will remind him not only that you're in charge, but also that everything he needs comes from you.

If your Pom continues to challenge your authority, especially if the power struggles escalate to the point that you become scared of him or he bites you, consult a behavior expert immediately to help you deal with this problem.

A dominant-aggressive dog often cannot be fully trusted around people because it's difficult to tell how the dog will respond in every situation. Certainly, a dog that's shown aggressive tendencies toward children should never be left alone with them, under any circumstances.

Chapter Six

Health and Nutrition

When it comes to keeping your Pomeranian in tip-top shape, mentally and physically, nothing surpasses the combination of good health care and proper nutrition. More than anything else, these two factors shape the dog your Pomeranian is right now—and the dog he will be in the years to come.

Your Pom's Veterinarian

Choosing a veterinarian for your Pomeranian can be difficult, unless you live somewhere so remote that only one is within a reasonable driving distance. More commonly, you'll have several choices or maybe even dozens. Some veterinarians specialize in certain species, such as dogs and cats. Others—especially those in urban areas—limit their practice to a clinical specialty, such as dermatology or surgery. Practice size varies too, from small clinics with just one veterinarian to large hospitals with ten or more.

Vaccinations

Vaccinations can protect your Pomeranian from many diseases. The most serious of these—rabies, distemper, infectious hepatitis, and parvovirus infection—are highly contagious and difficult to treat. All dogs need vaccinations against these diseases ("core" vaccinations). Other diseases, such as leptospirosis, kennel cough, and Lyme disease, are usually less serious and easier to treat. Only dogs at high risk of exposure need vaccinations for these diseases ("noncore" vaccinations). Your veterinarian can recommend the best vaccination schedule for your Pom.

BE PREPARED! How to Find a Veterinarian

Take the time to find a veterinarian who's just right for your Pom—and you. Here's how:

- Ask the breeder from whom you purchased your Pom.
- Ask your dog-owning friends which veterinarian they use.
- If you're moving to a new area, ask your current veterinarian to recommend a veterinarian in your new location.
- Contact the nearest college of veterinary medicine—they may be able to give you a list of veterinarians in your area.
- Check the online locating service of the American Animal Hospital Association, an organization of veterinarians (*www.healthypet.com*).
- Once you've found two or three veterinarians, make appointments to interview each one. Observe the veterinarian and staff at work, paying close attention to how they interact with the patients and their owners. Tour the hospital, if possible. Ask lots of questions—a good veterinarian will be happy to answer them.

Core Vaccinations

Rabies is a viral disease that can affect any mammal. It is most commonly contracted when saliva from an infected animal enters an open wound (usually a bite wound) and comes into contact with nerve endings. A dog with rabies may first demonstrate an unusual change in behavior. For instance, a previously shy dog may become friendly, or a good-natured dog may become nervous and reclusive. In the second stage of the disease, the dog becomes frenzied and hyperreactive (the origin of the terms *mad dog* and *furious rabies*). He may become very aggressive and attempt to bite inanimate or imaginary objects. In some cases, the dog becomes stuporous and oblivious to his surroundings (*dumb rabies*). In the final stages, the rabid dog becomes progressively paralyzed. Drooling ("foaming at the mouth") occurs because paralysis of the jaw muscles makes it difficult to swallow. Death usually occurs within 24 to 48 hours.

Distemper is a highly contagious viral disease that is spread primarily via body secretions (urine, feces, or nasal discharge) and by contact with contaminated objects such as brushes, blankets, and feed bowls. The incubation period for distemper is 14 to 18 days. Young, non-immunized dogs are highly susceptible.

A dog with distemper may at first have mild "cold"-like symptoms: slight fever, nasal discharge, and listlessness. As the disease progresses, the dog develops a pus-like discharge from the eyes and nose, as well as anorexia, vomiting, diarrhea, and coughing. In the later stages of distemper, the dog may show signs of acute encephalitis—seizures, muscle twitching, incoordi-

FYI: Core Vaccination Schedule

Disease	Initial Vaccination Series			Boosters	
	Start (age)	Revaccination	Until (age)	First (age)	Subsequent
Distemper*	6–8 wks	every 3–4 wks	16 wks	1 yr	every 3 yrs
Hepatitis*	6–8 wks	every 3–4 wks	16 wks	1 yr	every 3 yrs
Parvovirus*	6–8 wks	every 3–4 wks	18–20 wks	1 yr	every 3 yrs
Rabies	16 wks	none		1 yr	every 1 or 3 yrs**

* Dogs older than 16 weeks when initially vaccinated need only one revaccination 3–4 weeks later, then boosters as shown.
** Depends on local law.

nation, crying out, fearful behavior, circling, and blindness. The more severe the neurological problems are, the poorer the outlook for recovery.

Dogs that recover from distemper may have permanent neurological problems such as muscle spasms and impaired vision.

Infectious Hepatitis, a viral disease, most often occurs in young dogs. Most infections are inapparent, but the virus can cause a rapidly progressing, fatal disease that resembles distemper and parvovirus infection. Infected dogs shed the virus in all bodily secretions, including feces, urine, nasal secretions, saliva, and blood. Other dogs become infected when they inhale or ingest the virus. The incubation period for hepatitis is four to seven days.

Initially, the dog with hepatitis may have a rather high fever (103 to 106°F/40–41°C), which decreases within 24 hours. In mild cases, the dog recovers after one or two days. In moderate cases, the temperature does not decrease to normal and increases again in one or two days. The dog often becomes lethargic and anorexic. Other signs of severe hepatitis include small pinpoint hemorrhages (visible on the gums), vomiting, and bloody diarrhea, as well as abdominal tenderness and distension. In some dogs, coughing develops and progresses to pneumonia. When hepatitis affects multiple body systems, the prognosis is guarded. Dogs so afflicted may lapse into a coma and die, or may die from shock.

Parvovirus infections are often inapparent, but factors such as young age, stress, intestinal parasites, or bacterial infection may predispose a dog to severe disease. The principal signs of parvovirus infection are vomiting, diarrhea, lethargy, and anorexia. Severely affected dogs can develop persistent vomiting and bloody diarrhea, which can lead to death in less than 24 hours. A dog that recovers from parvovirus infection will have lifelong immunity.

Noncore Vaccinations

Leptospirosis is caused by a spiral-shaped bacteria called a spirochete. The organism is shed in the urine, which contaminates soil, water, and feed. Dogs become infected when they come into contact with infected urine or contaminated substances. Leptospirosis initially causes fever, vomiting, and anorexia. As the disease progresses, the dog may develop muscle soreness, bloody diarrhea, excessive thirst, excessive urination, and sores in the mouth. Jaundice occurs in some dogs, causing a yellowish coloration of the sclera (whites of the eyes), conjunctiva (linings of the eyelids), and mouth. Dogs that have recovered from leptospirosis can shed the infective organism for up to four years.

Vaccination for leptospirosis won't fully protect your Pom, because the vaccine protects only against the most common strains of the bacteria that cause the disease, rather than all of them. In addition, for unknown reasons some dogs fail to respond to the vaccine.

Kennel Cough (infectious tracheobronchitis) is a disease caused by several different organisms, including bacteria (especially *Bordetella bronchiseptica*) and viruses (especially parainfluenza virus). Though highly contagious, kennel cough is usually a mild, self-limiting disease. Infected dogs have mild to severe episodes of coughing, which may be aggravated by exercise, excitement, or pressure on the trachea. The cough may sound soft and moist, or harsh and dry. Infected dogs often gag at the end of a coughing episode,

FYI: Signs of Illness and Injury

Symptom	Examples	Notes
Unusual behavior	Listlessness, disinterest, irritability, unconsciousness, hyperactivity, seizures	Contact your veterinarian immediately if your Pom is unconscious or has a seizure.
Difficulty standing or moving around	Incoordination, stumbling, circling, limping, paralysis	Contact your veterinarian immediately if your Pom appears to be paralyzed.
Pain	Persistent whining, growling or aggression, reluctance to move, limping, hiding	Contact your veterinarian.
Obvious wound or injury	Cuts, puncture wounds, abscesses, broken bones	Contact your veterinarian immediately if your Pom is bleeding uncontrollably or appears to have a broken bone.
Change in eating or drinking behavior	Not eating, not drinking, excessive eating and drinking	Contact your veterinarian.
Respiratory abnormality	Coughing, sneezing, labored breathing, gasping	Contact your veterinarian immediately if your Pom's tongue or gums look blue, or he collapses.
Digestive tract abnormality	Vomiting, diarrhea, constipation	Contact your veterinarian.
Urinary tract abnormality	Blood in urine, absent or excessive urination, straining to urinate, housetraining "accidents"	Contact your veterinarian immediately if your Pom cannot urinate.
Secretion or discharge from nose, eyes, mouth or elsewhere	Mucus, watery fluid, pus, blood, or other secretions from nose, eyes, mouth, or elsewhere	Normal secretions are usually unnoticeable in healthy dogs.
Weight loss	Unexplained, not due to dietary restriction	Unexplained weight loss accompanies disorders such as internal parasites, diabetes, cancer, and many others.
Fever	Fever above 102.5°F	Normal canine body temperature: 100.5 to 102.5°F (38–39°C). Excitement or excessive activity can elevate body temperature.

which sometimes leads owners to mistakenly believe that their dog is vomiting. Most dogs with kennel cough are active and alert, with normal appetite and no fever. In rare cases—primarily in immunocompromised adults and unvaccinated puppies—the disease can cause fever, pneumonia, and death.

Recovery from kennel cough takes about two to three weeks. Dogs that have recovered from it may shed the infective organisms for more than three months. Some dogs become persistently infected carriers. Vaccination will decrease the incidence and severity of the disease, but not completely prevent it.

Lyme Disease is caused by *Borrelia burgdorferi*, which is carried by deer ticks. The disease, which may occur months after the infective tick bite, causes fever, weakness, joint pain, and lameness. The lameness may be transient, recurring at intervals as short as one month and as long as twenty-three months. If left untreated, Lyme disease can cause serious complications and even death.

Deer ticks are found primarily on certain species of deer and mice. It's often difficult to tell the difference between tiny deer ticks and immature forms of other ticks, which do not carry Lyme disease. The tick must feed for about 48 hours on the dog in order to cause infection. Lyme disease has been reported in nearly every state in the United States, but the incidence is highest on the Atlantic and Pacific coasts and the upper Midwest.

Helpful Hints

Temperature Check

Always use a plastic digital thermometer, never a glass one, when taking your Pom's temperature. To take his temperature, turn the thermometer on, place a dab of lubricant (K-Y Jelly or petroleum jelly) on the end, and gently insert it into the rectum to a depth of about 1 inch (2.5 cm). Hold the thermometer in place until the thermometer beeps to signal that it is finished.

Vaccination Reactions

Your Pom puppy may be listless and anorexic, with a low-grade fever, for about 24 hours after vaccination. Usually no treatment is necessary, other than sympathy and cuddles, but contact your veterinarian if he develops other signs (hives, itchiness, vomiting, diarrhea, difficulty breathing), which could indicate a more serious reaction.

Specific Health Problems

Identifying a health problem is the first step of taking care of it, whether that means administering first aid or taking your Pom to the veterinarian for diagnosis and treatment. Chances are your pal won't have a lot of health problems, but it helps to know a little about some of the more common ailments that might crop up.

Cuts and Bleeding

Cuts (lacerations) range in severity from minor to life-threatening, but most are minor. Even minor cuts can seem worse than they really are, because a small amount of blood, when smeared around, can look like a lot of blood. Blood from a vein is dark red and flows steadily. Blood from an artery is bright red and spurts. Arterial bleeding is usually more serious. To stop bleeding, apply gentle but firm pressure directly to the wound with a gauze pad, clean cloth, or towel. It's okay to secure the gauze or cloth with tape over the wound, but don't use a tourniquet, because it can cause pain and tissue damage if it's not used correctly.

Vomiting and Diarrhea

If your Pom vomits once, it's not usually cause for alarm, especially if he seems normal otherwise. Many dogs vomit occasionally, especially after eating grass or a very large meal. Similarly, an isolated episode of diarrhea is not unusual, especially if your Pom is nervous or has increased his water consumption because of hot weather. Repeated vomiting or diarrhea, however, could mean your guy has a more serious problem such as gastroenteritis, pancreatitis, or a gastrointestinal foreign body or other obstruction. Persistent vomiting and diarrhea can lead to electrolyte loss and dehydration, especially in young puppies.

If your Pom has repeated episodes of vomiting or diarrhea, he needs to be evaluated by your veterinarian as soon as possible. Don't give him any medication unless instructed to do so by your veterinarian.

Keep It Down If your Pom is vomiting, don't give him free access to food and water, which will probably cause more vomiting. If he seems thirsty, offer him a few ice cubes or ice chips instead of water.

Fractures (Broken Bones)

You may not be able to tell if your Pom has a fracture just by looking, especially if the injury involves the foot, the ribs, or head. If he's broken his leg, however, it will probably be so painful that he won't want to bear any weight on it at all. His leg may dangle oddly or appear to have an extra joint.

Some fractures are more serious than others. For example, skull fractures are always serious because of the possibility of brain injury. An open (compound) fracture—one that has an open wound—is more serious than a closed (simple) fracture, which has no open wound, because the risk of infection is greater.

If you think your Pom has a broken bone, take him to your veterinarian or emergency clinic as soon as possible. Don't try to bandage or splint the injury. Move your little pal gently and carefully to minimize movement of the broken bone. If he reacts violently to the pain, you may need to muzzle him to avoid being bitten.

Patellar Luxation

Patellar luxation, an inherited disorder in some Poms and other toy breeds, affects the stifle (knee) joint on the rear leg. Normally, the patella slides up and down in a groove on the femur as the dog bends and straightens the joint. In dogs with patellar luxation, the patella slips out of the groove, usually to the inner side of the leg in small-breed dogs. The severity of patellar luxation (and the lameness it causes) varies from Grade 1, in which the patella moves easily out and into place, to Grade 4, in which the patella is always displaced. The abnormal movement of the patella eventually damages the stifle joint, especially in severely affected dogs. Patellar luxation can be treated with surgery, which may involve a combination of procedures designed to maintain the normal configuration of the joint during movement.

Eye Problems

A Foreign Body (for example, grass, seed, grit, or a splinter) in your Pom's eye may or may not be painful, depending on the location of the object and whether it is embedded in the eye or surrounding structures.

If you suspect that your pal has something in his eye, gently pry his lids apart and take a look. Depending on his response, you might need to muzzle him and/or have someone hold him. Being careful not to touch the eye, gently flood it with warm water or eye-irrigating solution (such as Dacriose or Eye-Stream) dripped from a cotton ball. Repeat, if necessary. Use *only* this flooding technique—*do not* try to remove the foreign body with a cotton swab, gauze pad, or tissue. If you cannot wash the object out of the eye, take your Pom to your veterinarian as soon as possible.

Helpful Hints

Ouch!

Signs of eye pain include tearing, squinting, holding the lids tightly shut, and nervousness about being touched near the eye.

Conjunctivitis is an inflammation of the lining of the eyelids (the conjunctiva) and can be caused by local or generalized infection or by contact with irritating substances. If your Pom has conjunctivitis, his conjunctiva will be red and inflamed. Depending on the cause of the problem, he may have a mucous or pus-like discharge from the affected eye(s). The pain associated with conjunctivitis varies.

Corneal Injuries occur when the cornea—the clear outer covering of the eye—has been scratched or punctured. If your Pom has a corneal injury, he may vigorously resist your efforts to examine his eye—these injuries are often extremely painful. Some corneal injuries cannot be detected without special diagnostic techniques. In other cases, the cornea may appear cloudy over the injury.

A Cataract is a cloudiness of the lens of the eye. If your buddy has a cataract, you may be able to see the cloudiness when you look directly into

BE PREPARED! Giving Medication

Oral Medication: Pills and liquids are the most common forms of oral medication. To give your Pom a pill the easy way, place the medication in a small ball of wet dog food or a piece of soft cheese and offer it as a treat. This will work well if he wants the goodie, but if he doesn't, you'll have to resort to other tactics. First, tuck your buddy under your left arm (if you're right-handed; if you're left-handed, reverse these instructions). Bring your left hand up on his left side over his head and grasp his muzzle. With the other hand (holding the pill) on the lower jaw, gently tilt his head up. His mouth will probably open slightly. With the fingers of your right hand, open his mouth more widely and quickly place the pill on the middle of his tongue as far back as you can. Close his mouth and hold it shut, then rub his throat and tell him what a good dog he is. After about a minute, let him open his mouth. If he spits the pill out, try again.

To give liquid medication, put it in a syringe (with no needle) or plastic eye-dropper. Offer your Pom a few drops of the medication—many are flavored, so he may just lap it on his own. If he doesn't, tilt his head up and insert the syringe or dropper in the corner of his mouth between his cheek and teeth. Slowly dribble the liquid into his mouth. He'll probably swallow the medication without much fuss.

Eye Medication: Eye medication usually comes in ointment or drop form. When administering either type, it's important to avoid touching the eye with the applicator or your fingers. Most dogs tolerate ointment application better than eyedrops.

To apply ointment, gently pull your Pom's lower eyelid down and deposit a blob of ointment inside it. Close the eyelids with your fingers to distribute the ointment.

To apply drops, tilt your Pom's head up, hold the eyelids apart, and quickly deposit the drops in the inside corner of the eye or inside the lower eyelid. Hold the dropper close to his eye—you'll be less likely to miss your target and it will be more comfortable for your pal.

Ear Medication: To apply ear medication (ointment or drops), tilt your Pom's head to the side with the affected ear up and place the medication into the ear canal. He may try to shake his head afterward, so hold it securely while you gently massage the ear to help distribute the medication.

Topical Medication: Topical medications, which are applied to the skin, are usually ointments, but sometimes they're liquids. You can apply ointment directly to your Pom's skin, or put a little on your finger and then apply it. Drops are usually applied directly to the skin. After applying either type of medication, rub it in well (unless otherwise instructed by your veterinarian). Your greatest difficulty with topical medication will probably be keeping your Pom from licking it off. Try some distraction tactics: Take your buddy for a walk or play with him until he loses interest in trying to remove the medication.

his eyes. Severe cataracts can cause blindness. In some cases, surgical removal of the affected lens can restore at least partial vision.

Many older dogs develop sclerosis of the lens, which, like cataracts, makes the eyes look hazy, but usually requires no treatment.

Glaucoma is a disorder that causes excessive pressure within the eyeball. The increased pressure eventually damages the internal structures of the eye, causing blindness. Glaucoma can sometimes be treated successfully with medication. In advanced cases, removal of the eye may be necessary.

If your Pom has an eye problem, even if it seems to be minor, he should be evaluated by your veterinarian. Prompt treatment may save his sight. Other than flooding the eye to remove minor foreign bodies, never attempt any type of home treatment for an eye problem unless directed to do so by your veterinarian.

Ear Problems

The most common canine ear problem is otitis externa, inflammation of the external ear canal. Otitis externa has many causes: foreign bodies (foxtails, grass awns, etc.), ear mites, irritation, and excessive moisture. Allergies—to food or inhaled substances—are a common, but often overlooked, cause. Secondary bacterial or yeast infections often complicate otitis externa. If your Pom develops otitis externa, he may repeatedly shake his head or scratch the affected ear, which may have a discharge and bad smell. As soon as you notice these symptoms, take your pal to your veterinarian for diagnosis and treatment. If untreated, the inflammation/infection can extend into the middle or inner ear and cause serious complications.

Heart Disease

Some heart diseases are characterized by structural abnormalities, such as defects between adjacent chambers of the heart or malpositioning of the vessels around the heart. One of these diseases, patent ductus arteriosus, occurs in some Pomeranians. Before birth, the ductus arteriosus connects the pulmonary artery (the blood vessel that takes blood from the heart to the lungs) and the aorta (the blood vessel that takes blood from the heart to the body). The blood bypasses the lungs, which don't function until after birth. Normally, the ductus arteriosus closes within a few days of birth, but in some puppies it remains open. The resulting abnormal blood flow (usually from the aorta into the pulmonary artery) can damage the lungs and heart and eventually lead to heart failure. Patent ductus arteriosus can be surgically corrected—a lifesaving procedure, since more than half of the puppies affected, if not treated, will die within one year.

Some types of heart disease develop later in the dog's life. The most common of these is mitral insufficiency, in which one of the heart valves does not close properly and allows some of the blood to flow backward instead of forward. Many cases of mitral insufficiency can be well-managed with proper medication.

The symptoms of heart disease vary depending on the specific condition and its severity, but often include lethargy, shortness of breath, coughing, abdominal distension, and exercise intolerance.

Skin Problems

Skin problems have many causes, including external parasites (fleas, ticks, and mites), allergies, endocrine diseases, and bacterial and yeast/fungal infections. Depending on the condition, the skin may be dry and scaly or moist and oozing. The problem may be generalized, as with allergies, or localized, as with fungal infections such as ringworm. Hair loss, when present, may occur in just one area or all over the body. Itching (pruritus), which may be severe, occurs with many skin problems. The resulting self-trauma increases the likelihood of secondary bacterial or yeast infections.

If your Pom develops a skin problem that's more than an uncomplicated case of fleas or ticks, don't try to treat it yourself. Given the diversity of skin

Breed Truths

Alopecia X

Alopecia X is a disorder that causes hair loss—without itching, inflammation, or secondary infections—in some Pomeranians and other plush-coated breeds. This unusual skin problem may stem from an inherited adrenal gland defect that causes abnormal levels of sex hormones and possibly an abnormality of hormone receptors on the hair follicles. Since Alopecia X is solely cosmetic, most veterinarians don't recommend aggressive treatment. Spaying or neutering often causes hair regrowth, which may be permanent. Medications affecting adrenal function or the hair growth cycle don't work as well and may have undesirable side effects.

FYI: Allergy Attack

Different allergies often cause the same skin symptoms—redness and itching—but it's not always easy to tell what's causing the allergy. The major culprits are usually fleas, inhaled substances, and foods.

Fleas Flea bite allergy is the number one allergy in dogs. Since the allergen is contained in flea saliva, it only takes a few bites to cause a generalized reaction in a susceptible dog. Finding fleas on a dog with allergy symptoms obviously suggests that they are the cause, but the dog may have other allergies as well. The fleas must be eliminated in order to effectively treat flea bite allergy.

Inhaled Substances The list of possible triggers for this type of allergy (also called atopy) is extensive: pollens, molds, house dust, and many others. Some dogs have only seasonal symptoms; others suffer all year long. Some dogs have an inherited predisposition for atopy. Skin testing may be necessary to pinpoint the triggering allergen(s). Treatment involves avoidance of the triggering substance and a variety of medications, including topical ointments or sprays, antihistamines, corticosteroids, immunosuppressants, and hyposensitization ("allergy shots"). A combination of therapies is often the most effective.

Foods Most food allergies cause skin problems rather than digestive tract symptoms, such as vomiting or diarrhea. Common trigger foods include beef, dairy products, chicken, lamb, and eggs, but many others can also cause allergic reactions. The most effective way to diagnose a food allergy is by feeding a special diet (elimination diet) made up of only one protein and one carbohydrate that the dog has never eaten, for at least eight weeks. Single ingredients are then systematically added until the allergy symptoms recur, indicating the triggering ingredient, which can then be eliminated from the diet.

problems and high incidence of secondary infections, it's important to rely on your veterinarian to diagnose the primary cause and secondary infections (if any), and prescribe the necessary treatment.

Cancer

About 45 percent of all dogs over 10 years of age die from cancer. The disease takes many forms. Some cancers are easy to see and look like nodules, lumps, or sores. Other cancers are internal and can be detected only with special diagnostic techniques. Cancer often causes symptoms that mimic another disease.

The outlook for a dog with cancer varies, depending on the type and size of tumor, the duration of illness, whether it has metastasized (spread to other areas of the body), and the treatment chosen. In the past 10 years, much progress has been made in the diagnosis and treatment of cancer in animals. Treatment options include surgical removal, chemotherapy, and radiation therapy. These treatments are often combined to produce a higher rate of remission or cure.

Poisoning

Substances that are poisonous to dogs range from seemingly innocuous compounds such as chocolate to more obvious poisons such as strychnine. Most poisonings occur when the dog eats a toxic substance, but they can also occur by skin contact or inhalation.

Symptoms of poisoning vary widely because of the great diversity of toxic substances. Some poisons cause vomiting, others do not. A dog that has been poisoned may be lethargic or even comatose, or it may be restless or agitated. Progressively severe seizures may occur with some poisons. To further complicate things, many other diseases cause symptoms that are similar to those of poisoning.

If you think your Pom has been poisoned, contact your veterinarian or emergency clinic immediately. If you know what he was exposed to, tell your veterinarian, and provide any label or container information, if available. Do not administer any treatment or medication, unless instructed to do so by your veterinarian.

Heatstroke

Dogs cool themselves by panting—a less efficient means of temperature control than sweating. Heatstroke occurs when a dog cannot get rid of excess body heat. Predisposing factors include a heavy coat, obesity, excessive activity, and confinement in a poorly ventilated, warm environment.

One of the most common causes of heatstroke in dogs is confinement in a car on a warm day. *Never* leave your Pom in a closed car, even on a mild day—the temperature in the car can quickly become dangerously high.

SHOPPING LIST

First-Aid Kit Essentials

- ✔ Veterinarian's phone number
- ✔ Emergency clinic phone number
- ✔ Poison Control Hotline phone number
- ✔ Nylon leash
- ✔ Muzzle
- ✔ Roll gauze
- ✔ Gauze pads (some sterile)
- ✔ Nonstick dressing pads
- ✔ Adhesive tape
- ✔ Nonstick self-adhesive tape
- ✔ Wound disinfectant (such as Betadine or Novalsan solution)
- ✔ Scissors
- ✔ Tweezers
- ✔ Needle-nose pliers or hemostat
- ✔ Eyedropper or oral syringe
- ✔ Nutritional supplement paste (such as Nutri-Cal)
- ✔ Hydrogen peroxide
- ✔ Activated charcoal or milk of magnesia
- ✔ Towels or other soft cloths
- ✔ "Stretcher" (small board or towel)

Heatstroke will make your Pom depressed and lethargic. His body temperature will be extremely high—sometimes as high as 106°F (39°C)—and his ears and mouth may actually feel hot to the touch. Signs of shock—high heart rate, high respiratory rate, pale gums, and collapse—may be present. Heatstroke can be fatal, so immediate veterinary care is necessary.

Emergency procedures that will help lower your Pom's body temperature include wetting down his coat with cool (not cold) water, placing an ice pack (wrapped in a washcloth) in the groin area, and offering cold water or ice chips, if he's conscious.

Internal Parasites

Internal parasites are common inhabitants of dogs of all ages. Sometimes these freeloaders cause few, if any, clinical symptoms. In other cases, particularly in young puppies or dogs afflicted with pre-existing health problems, they can cause serious or even life-threatening illness.

Heartworms

Not all internal parasites infect the gastrointestinal system. Heartworms live in the heart and in some of the large blood vessels around the heart. This parasite, which is spread by mosquitoes, occurs throughout the United States. The cycle starts when a female mosquito ingests immature infective heartworms (microfilariae) while feeding on an infected dog. The immature microfilariae develop within the mosquito, which eventually introduces them into another dog while feeding. After migrating through the dog's body, the larval heartworms eventually end up in the arteries of the lungs, where they develop further and produce microfilariae. The entire cycle takes about six months. At first, the adult heartworms live only in the blood vessels of the lungs, but as they multiply, they move into the vessels between the heart and the lungs, and eventually the heart itself.

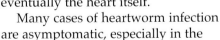

CAUTION

Good sanitation is important for the control of all intestinal parasites, especially in situations where large numbers of dogs are housed together. Floors of kennels and runs should be impervious and easily cleaned and disinfected. Regular feces removal, preventing fecal contamination of food and water, and disinfecting bowls and utensils daily will also help decrease parasite infection.

Many cases of heartworm infection are asymptomatic, especially in the early stages or in sedentary dogs. As the disease progresses, coughing, shortness of breath, and exercise intolerance occur. Severe heartworm infection can ultimately cause heart failure and death.

Heartworm infections must be treated with two types of medication—first, a medication to kill the adult heartworms and, four to six weeks later, another medication to kill the microfilariae. Monthly treatment with an oral medication such as ivermectin will prevent heartworm infection. At least one preventive (selamectin) is available as a topical "spot-on"—a liquid that you apply to a small area of the skin. The medications in some heartworm preventives also treat and prevent certain intestinal parasites.

Puppies can be started on heartworm preventive as early as four weeks of age, but must be tested for heartworms six months to one year later. If your Pom is older than six months of age, he should be tested for heartworms before you start him on preventive. After that, he'll need to be retested every one to three years to make sure he didn't become infected before starting the preventive or while he was taking the preventive (especially if he didn't get all his doses). Some heartworm preventives occasionally cause allergic-type reactions in dogs with preexisting heartworm infection. Symptoms usually involve digestive tract upset, especially diarrhea, but in rare cases shock and even death can occur.

If you live in a warm climate, you'll need to give your Pom heartworm preventive medication year-round. If you live in an area with a seasonal climate, you may be able to stop giving the preventive during the winter months. Check with your veterinarian to find out which preventive your Pom needs, how long you should give it, and when your little friend should be tested for heartworms.

Treatment for heartworms, especially the adults, is always risky. The adults remain in the body after they die, slowly breaking up into progressively smaller segments, which are gradually eliminated by white blood cells. Segments that are swept away in the bloodstream may cause pulmonary thromboembolism, which can be life-threatening. Symptoms include low-grade fever, coughing (sometimes with blood), shortness of breath, and heart failure. Physical activity increases the risk of pulmonary thromboembolism, so dogs that have been treated for adult heartworms should not exercise more vigorously than walking for about four to six weeks after treatment.

Roundworms

Roundworms are the most common canine internal parasite. Dogs of all ages can become infected when they ingest the eggs, which are found mainly in the soil. In puppies, the roundworm larvae migrate to the lungs, where they are coughed up and swallowed. They then pass into the small intestine to develop into adults. In adult dogs, the larvae migrate to the muscles, kidneys, and other body tissues, where they become dormant. Pregnancy activates the dormant larvae, which migrate to the placenta or mammary glands to infect the puppies prior to birth or when they nurse.

Roundworm larvae can also infect humans and migrate through the body (*visceral larval migrans*) or eye (*ocular larval migrans*).

Adult dogs often show no symptoms of roundworm infection. In puppies, the symptoms include abdominal pain and distension, diarrhea, stunted growth, and dull coat. Severely affected puppies may develop pneumonia due to the migration of the larval roundworms through the lungs.

Roundworms are diagnosed with a fecal flotation test, a laboratory procedure used to examine a stool sample for parasite eggs. Adult roundworms are also occasionally found in the stool or vomit. Medication for roundworm infestation is usually quite safe and can be administered to puppies as young as two weeks of age. More than one treatment is often necessary to completely eliminate the parasites. Controlling roundworms in adult dogs, especially breeding females, and in the environment will decrease infections in the puppies. Some heartworm preventive medications also control roundworms.

Hookworms

Hookworms are bloodsucking intestinal parasites that are found in dogs of all ages. Infection can occur by ingestion of the larvae or by larval penetration of the skin.

Many of these larvae make their way to the small intestine, where they develop into adults. Some travel to the lungs, where they are coughed up, swallowed, and wind up in the small intestine. Still others become dormant while migrating through various body tissues. During pregnancy, the dormant larvae become active again and migrate to the placenta or mammary glands where they infect the puppies prior to or shortly after birth.

Some types of hookworm larvae can infect humans and migrate under the skin (*cutaneous larval migrans*) or into the intestines (*eosinophilic enteritis*).

Symptoms of hookworm infection in puppies include blood loss, diarrhea (sometimes tarry or bloody), pale gums, anemia, weakness, and emaciation.

Hookworms are diagnosed with a fecal flotation test. Various medications are effective against the parasite, but more than one treatment may be needed. As with roundworms, controlling hookworms in breeding females will decrease infections in the puppies. Some heartworm preventive medications also control hookworms.

Whipworms

Whipworms are commonly found in the colon and cecum of dogs of all ages. Infection occurs when the dog ingests the infective eggs. Most whipworm infections are asymptomatic, but some dogs may develop chronic or intermittent diarrhea. Because the female whipworm sheds eggs sporadically, several fecal flotation tests may be needed to diagnose the infection. Various medications are effective against whipworms, and some heartworm preventive medications will also control them. The eggs are quite resistant in the environment, so frequent treatment of runs and kennels may be necessary to prevent reinfection.

Tapeworms

The most common type of tapeworm infection in dogs occurs when the dog ingests infected intermediate hosts—fleas and lice. A less common species of tapeworm is carried by rodents, rabbits, sheep, and cattle.

Tapeworms cause few symptoms in dogs, but some may experience a slight weight loss.

Intact tapeworms are long and flat, with a body that is divided into infective segments called proglottids, which are shed in the feces. Tapeworms are most frequently diagnosed when the owner sees the white, mobile, rice-sized proglottids in the dog's anal area, feces, or bedding.

Treatment of tapeworm infection involves eliminating both the parasites and the intermediate hosts. Thus, flea and lice control and prevention of scavenging and hunting are important aspects of effective treatment.

Coccidia

The term coccidia does not refer to a single parasite, but rather to any of a group of six protozoan parasites. Infection occurs when the dog ingests infective "egg packets" (oocysts) or oocyst-containing raw meat or rodents and other prey.

Coccidia infection usually causes no clinical symptoms, especially in healthy adult dogs. In puppies, coccidia infection in the presence of high stress, poor sanitation, overcrowding, malnutrition, and concurrent immunosuppressive diseases (such as distemper) can cause diarrhea, vomiting, listlessness, weight loss, and dehydration.

Infection is diagnosed by fecal flotation. Treatment is indicated if clinical signs are present, especially in newborn puppies or compromised dogs of any age. Prevention of scavenging and hunting, and elimination of raw meat from the diet will reduce the likelihood of infection.

External Parasites

No one likes to think about bugs living on their dog, but that's exactly what external parasites do. Fleas, ticks, and other pests can torment your Pom with their crawling and biting, no doubt about it, but that's not all. They can also induce allergies, cause dermatitis, and, in some cases, transmit some rather nasty diseases.

Fleas

Fleas are the most common parasite of dogs. The adults—the only ones that bite—spend most of their time on the dog. They lay their eggs there, but the eggs quickly fall off, landing on the dog bed (or your bed), carpet, or furniture. When the eggs hatch, the immature fleas feed on organic debris and flea excrement. When they become adults, they hop back onto the dog to feed on blood and reproduce.

Helpful Hints

Out They Go!

Put moth balls/crystals, flea powder, or a few pieces of a flea collar in the vacuum bag or canister to kill vacuumed-up fleas and larvae. After vacuuming, remove the bag, seal it in a plastic garbage bag, and throw it away in an outside trash container.

Fleas torment dogs in a number of ways. Their feeding and movement causes localized itching and inflammation. Some dogs become allergic to substances in flea saliva and develop generalized dermatitis. Severe flea infestation can cause anemia because of chronic blood loss, especially in puppies or older dogs with concurrent disease. Fleas also transmit one type of tapeworm to dogs.

If you think your Pom has fleas, but can't seem to spot them, take a close look at his neck, abdomen, and tail base—areas where fleas like to hang out. Even if you don't see the actual critters, you may see flea excrement—dark, reddish-brown stuff that looks like specks of dirt.

Flea control can be difficult, since fleas can survive for long periods of time in the environment, especially under warm, humid conditions. Treatment is twofold: eliminating the fleas on your Pom and eliminating them from the areas where your Pom has been—your home and yard.

The most effective flea control products—available in collars, oral medications, sprays, and spot-ons—disrupt the flea life cycle by killing the adult fleas and/or the eggs that have been laid on the dog.

Thorough vacuuming will eliminate some of the flea eggs and larvae in your home. It also removes flea excrement and stimulates young adult fleas to leave their protective cocoons, which makes them vulnerable to pesticides. In addition to vacuuming, wash your Pom's bedding and anything else he sleeps on, if possible. To get rid of even more fleas, apply a household insecticide designed for that purpose.

If your Pom spends time in your yard, you'll need to treat it with a suitable yard spray, preferably one that combines an insecticide and insect growth regulator. You don't have to treat your entire yard, just your Pom's favorite resting spots (especially if they're cool and shady) and paths.

If you still have a flea problem after you've treated your Pom, your house, and your yard, consult a professional exterminator.

HOME BASICS
Removing Ticks

To remove a tick, grasp it with your fingers or tweezers as close to the skin as possible and slowly pull it off. Don't worry if part of the head stays embedded—this usually just causes a local reaction that will clear up on its own. When you're done, wash the spot—and your hands—with mild antiseptic soap.

Ticks

Ticks not only bite, but can cause anemia (especially in puppies) and transmit serious diseases such as Rocky Mountain spotted fever, Lyme disease, and ehrlichiosis to dogs and people. Dogs become infested with ticks when they brush against grass and foliage where larval ticks ("seed ticks") congregate. The immature ticks go through several stages of feeding and molting as they develop. Finally, the adult females feed and breed, after which they drop off the dog to lay thousands of eggs and die. When the eggs hatch, the larval ticks move to the grass and foliage and the cycle is repeated.

Controlling ticks can be difficult, but newer products on the market make it easier and safer than it used to be. Some spot-on products repel and kill ticks—and control fleas and sometimes mosquitoes—for 30 days after one application. Some tick collars are effective for three months. Regardless of which product you choose for your Pom, be sure to use the old-fashioned method of tick control: checking your furry friend for ticks every day.

As with fleas, complete tick control involves treating your yard as well as your Pom. To eliminate tick hiding places, keep your lawn mowed and free from overgrown brush. Keep tick-bearing wildlife, such as deer, out of your yard. Spraying your yard with a product specifically designed for tick control (many control fleas as well) will keep the critters at bay for about four weeks.

Tick Paralysis Some ticks can cause paralysis in dogs when they inject salivary toxins during prolonged feeding (four days or more). A single tick—especially if it's on or near the head—can cause the paralysis. The rear quarters are affected first, and then the paralysis spreads forward. The dog can die if the respiratory muscles become paralyzed. Fortunately, once the offending tick is removed, most dogs recover rapidly.

Mites

Demodex canis mites normally inhabit canine skin, but don't usually cause problems if the dog's immune system is functioning normally. Puppies sometimes develop small red hairless patches (localized demodicosis) that usually go away without treatment. If the Demodex mites multiply unchecked, however, they can cause generalized demodicosis (demodectic mange), with widespread itching, hair loss, and skin inflammation. Secondary bacterial and fungal infections make the itching and inflammation worse and complicate treatment. Treatment of generalized demodicosis involves treating the condition that allowed the mites to multiply, the mite infestation, and any underlying secondary infections. Veterinarians often prescribe oral anti-mite medication and medicated dips for the primary disease; oral antibiotic and antifungal medications are used to treat the secondary infections. Successful treatment is difficult and may take four months or longer. In some cases, especially in older dogs, the disease cannot be cured, only controlled.

Sarcoptes scabiei mites cause sarcoptic mange (scabies). The parasites burrow into the dog's skin, where they cause intense irritation and itching. Dried blood and serum encrust the inflamed skin, which eventually becomes wrinkled and thickened. Hair loss is widespread. Treatment for sarcoptic mange is similar to that for generalized demodicosis. People can contract sarcoptic mange from dogs, but this is relatively rare.

Ear mites live in the external ear canal, where they cause inflammation and severe itching. A dog with ear mites may abrade the skin of the head and ears by scratching and head rubbing. Sometimes the infected dog shakes his head so violently that it causes an aural hematoma, an injury in which blood accumulates between the cartilage and skin of the ear flap. Ear mites typically turn the earwax dark brown so the ear looks like it has dirt or dried blood inside it. Your veterinarian can tell if your Pom has ear mites by looking in his ears with an otoscope. When warmed by the light of the otoscope, the mites move around, which makes it easy to see them. If the diagnosis is positive, you'll need to treat all the dogs and cats in your household, because ear mites move readily from animal to animal.

Nutrition Needs

Your Pomeranian's well-being depends on proper nutrition as well as good veterinary care. Because of this—and the enthusiasm he likely has for tasty food—it's worth it to take the time to find the very best food for your furry friend.

Necessary Nutrients

All dog food contains a mixture of protein, carbohydrates, and fat, as well as essential vitamins and minerals. How these components are combined determines the nutritional balance of the food.

Proteins are made up of amino acids, ten of which must be supplied in the diet (essential amino acids). Proteins are used to grow and repair muscles, bones, and other body tissues. They are also essential for the production of antibodies, enzymes, and hormones. The best sources of proteins are meat, meat by-products, meat meal, eggs, dairy products, and soybeans. Proteins cannot be stored in the body; excessive amounts are metabolized into glucose and used for energy, or eliminated in the urine.

Carbohydrates are the major source of glucose, the body's primary energy supply. The preferred types of carbohydrates for canine diets are starches and fiber (cellulose), which are found in cereal grains, vegetables, and other plant products. Starches must be cooked in order to be digested.

Fiber is indigestible but aids in digestive tract function. Excess carbohy-drates are stored in the liver or muscles as glycogen, or converted to fat.

Fats are used for energy when carbohydrates are unavailable (as in dietary restriction) or metabolically unusable (as in diabetes mellitus). They are also essential for hormone function; nervous system function; transport of vitamins A, D, E, and K; coat and skin health; and maintenance of body temperature in cold climates. Fats also increase the palatability of food. Fat sources in dog foods include tallow, lard, poultry fat, fish oil, and vegetable oils. Fat is readily stored in the body.

Vitamins and Minerals are necessary for muscle and nerve function, bone growth, healing, metabolism, and fluid balance. They are found in a wide variety of plant and animal sources. Complete and balanced dog foods provide all the necessary vitamins and minerals. Unless advised by your veterinarian, there's no need to supplement your Pom's diet with added vitamins and minerals. Excessive amounts of some vitamins and minerals can be toxic.

Water

In addition to protein, carbohydrates, fats, vitamins, and minerals, your Pom also needs an unlimited supply of fresh clean water. Water is an essential component of every function of your pal's body. He can't store water in his body and has only limited means for conserving it. He needs at least 1 ounce (30 ml) of water per pound (.45 kg) of body weight every day—and much more than that in hot weather or when he's been exercising vigorously.

Types of Dog Food

Commercial dog food is available in four general types: dry, wet, semi-moist, and frozen. Each type has advantages and disadvantages, which you'll need to consider when choosing your Pom's food. If necessary, try different products, or even a combination: it won't take long before you find the food that's "just right" for your pal.

Dry Food (Kibble)

Dry food, the least expensive type of dog food, has several advantages: it takes longer to eat, so dogs may feel fuller; if fed dry, it satisfies the "urge to chew"; and it may promote dental health. Unmoistened dry food is suitable for free-choice feeding because it can be left out at room temperature without spoiling. On the downside, some dogs find dry food less appealing than other products. Others enjoy it, especially if they've eaten it exclusively since puppyhood.

Dry food requires more storage space than the other types of dog food. It should be stored in a cool, dry, bug- and vermin-free environment. For storage convenience, choose a product with a resealable bag. If the package isn't resealable, fold down the top and secure it with a clip or store the kibble in a food-grade, airtight plastic container.

Wet Food

Wet food is available in both cans and pouches. It is highly palatable and provides concentrated nutrition, which makes it useful for underweight dogs or for those recovering from illness. You can also add a little bit of wet food to dry food in order to increase the latter's appeal. Wet food cannot be used for free-choice feeding because it will spoil if left out. Feeding a diet of only wet food may increase your Pom's risk for periodontal disease. It will probably also turn him into a rather picky eater, at least for dry food.

Neither canned nor pouched wet food need to be refrigerated if unopened. Most wet food has an expiration date, so it's important to check the label for this information. Be sure to discard any puffy or leaky cans; they can harbor bacteria, which can make your dog very sick. Leftover wet food should be covered (cans) or resealed securely (pouches), refrigerated, and used within three days.

Semi-Moist Food

Semi-moist food is highly palatable and doesn't spoil when left out at room temperature. These features are primarily due to high levels of sugars and preservatives, which increase the risk of obesity and dental disorders. Because of this, semi-moist food is not a good choice for your Pom's primary diet. It's okay to use it for occasional treats, but remember to figure those treat calories into your Pom's daily caloric intake.

Semi-moist food doesn't need to be refrigerated. Be sure to securely reseal the pouch for storage.

Frozen Food

Frozen food, the most expensive type of dog food, is available as both cooked and raw products. Like wet food, it is highly palatable and provides concentrated nutrition, which makes it useful for underweight dogs or those recovering from illness. It can also be mixed with dry food to make the kibble more appetizing. Frozen food is usually preservative-free, which makes it highly perishable and not suited for free-choice feeding. Raw products are not recommended because of the risk of contracting various diseases and parasites.

Frozen food can be stored for at least one year in the freezer. The quality and the taste of the food may deteriorate with longer storage. Frozen food can be thawed in the refrigerator or in the microwave on the defrost setting. Any leftovers should be covered, refrigerated, and used within 24 hours.

Understanding the Label

All dog food labels contain the same information in pretty much the same format, but unfortunately this doesn't mean that the information is easy to understand. Here's how to decipher that label, so you can pick the best food for your Pom.

Dog foods labeled as "complete and balanced" must meet nutritional requirements set by the Association of American Feed Control Officials (AAFCO) for adults (maintenance) or puppies and pregnant/lactating bitches (growth and reproduction). All complete and balanced dog foods—including foods for seniors, weight management, specific breeds, or sizes—fall into at least one of these two categories.

The nutritional analysis lists the minimum amount ("not less than") of protein and fat, and the maximum amount ("not more than") of fiber and moisture (water). Carbohydrate content isn't listed because it's everything that's not protein, fat, fiber, or water. The values listed in the nutritional analysis are calculated on an "as fed" basis, meaning the food just as it comes from the package or can, without anything added. "Crude protein" and "crude fat" are determined by a machine in a laboratory. The values are technically accurate, but don't tell you anything about digestibility—how much of the nutrient your Pom can actually use. Ingredients are listed on the label in descending order of weight. Manufacturers often list separately different forms of a single ingredient (such as cornmeal and corn middlings), which can make it seem like that ingredient makes up a smaller proportion of the food than it actually does.The ingredient list shows what preservatives, if any, the food contains. Many manufacturers now include so-called "natural" preservatives such as mixed tocopherols (vitamin E) and vitamin C. Other foods contain no preservatives at all.

Dog Food Ingredients

Meat should appear near the top of the ingredient list, but you don't need to worry if you also see vegetables and even grains (corn, barley, rice, etc.), as long as the food is nutritionally complete and balanced. Dogs are omnivores—not carnivores, as many people think—and need some plant-derived nutrients for a balanced diet. Wolves and other wild *canidae* obtain these nutrients when they prey on herbivorous animals and eat plants, such as grass.

Feeding Plans

Wolves and other wild canine relatives eat when food is available, sometimes going for days between meals. Your Pom, however, will appreciate regular daily meals. How you provide those meals will depend on the feeding plan that you choose.

Free-Choice Feeding

With a free-choice feeding plan, the owner provides an amount of food that exceeds the dog's daily requirements; the dog determines how much and when to eat. Only dry food or semi-moist food is suitable for this feeding plan, since these products can be left out for long periods without spoiling. Free-choice feeding is simple for the owner, since there's no schedule to follow, and good for the dog that likes to nibble throughout the day.

Some dogs adapt readily to free-choice feeding, but others overeat and become overweight. This plan also makes it difficult to accurately determine how much the dog is eating. For example, if your Pom loses his appetite because of an illness, you might not detect it until he starts losing weight. Free-choice feeding complicates housetraining, because the irregular eating schedule makes it difficult to predict when your Pom will need to visit the "potty spot."

Breed Truths

Table Food

Feeding your Pom too much table food can unbalance his diet, lead to weight problems, and turn him into a picky eater. To avoid these problems, limit your Pom's intake of table food to 10 percent or less of his daily caloric intake.

BE PREPARED! What Not to Feed

The following food items can make your Pom sick—or worse:

- **Onions, garlic, and related foods:** can irritate the digestive tract and cause anemia if eaten in sufficient quantity.
- **Grapes, raisins:** can cause kidney failure. Toxicity varies from dog to dog.
- **Chocolate:** contains theobromine and methylxanthines, caffeine-like compounds that can cause vomiting, diarrhea, abnormal heartbeat, tremors, seizures, and death. Toxicity increases with the darkness of the chocolate.
- **Milk:** can cause diarrhea in adults and puppies.
- **Baby food:** Some products contain onion powder (see above).
- **Yeast bread dough:** can rise in gastrointestinal tract, causing obstruction and producing alcohol.
- **Macadamia nuts:** cause vomiting, weakness, incoordination, and other symptoms.
- **Avocados:** if eaten in sufficient quantity, can irritate the digestive tract and cause vomiting and diarrhea.
- **Raw eggs:** Raw egg white contains an enzyme that blocks the uptake of biotin, a B vitamin; raw eggs may contain salmonella.
- **Raw meat:** may expose your Pom to parasites and harmful bacteria such as *Salmonella* or *E. coli*.
- **Bones:** Raw bones can damage your Pom's teeth, cause digestive tract obstruction and perforation, and expose him to *Salmonella*, *E. coli*, and other harmful bacteria; cooked bones can cause severe constipation.

Time-Controlled Feeding

With time-controlled feeding, the owner offers a surplus of food for a predetermined period of time, usually 15 to 20 minutes. The dog eats as much as he wants within this time period, and then the food is taken away. All types of dog food are suitable for time-controlled feeding, since the food is not left out for more than 20 minutes. This feeding plan allows the dog to self-regulate his intake, but over a shorter period of time than with free-choice feeding. Overeating is less of a problem with dogs on a time-controlled feeding plan than with those that are fed free-choice. It's also easier to determine the amount of food your Pom has eaten. The predictable eating schedule makes housetraining easier.

Time-controlled feeding is not a good choice for dogs that prefer to nibble throughout the day or for those that overeat if given the opportunity.

Portion-Controlled Feeding

With a portioned-controlled feeding plan, the owner offers a predetermined amount of food (for example, one meal) and the dog decides when to eat it. This is a good plan for dogs that like to "graze" throughout the day. It gives the owner the most control over the amount of food eaten, which makes it easier to detect any changes in food intake.

Because of the lack of a regular eating schedule, portion-controlled feeding makes housetraining difficult. Since the food is left out for an indefinite period of time, this feeding plan is suitable only for dry and semi-moist food.

One Scoop or Two?

The amount of food your Pom needs each day depends on several factors, such as the age, activity level, metabolic rate, food quality, and the size of your Pom.

Age On a per-pound basis, puppies need more food than adults. Senior dogs often need less food than they did when they were younger, but sometimes they need more.

Activity Level A Pom that's always on the go burns more calories than one with a couch potato lifestyle.

Metabolic Rate Some Poms just seem to have higher metabolic rates than others, so they need more food.

Food Quality The high-quality ingredients found in premium dog foods are more digestible, so your Pom will need to eat less than if you fed him a "bargain" food.

Size A larger Pom usually needs more food than a smaller one, if the other factors are similar.

You don't have to be a nutrition expert to figure out how much food your buddy needs to stay in tip-top shape. Simply start by feeding him the amount of food recommended by the manufacturer (check the package label), and then adjust it as needed. For example, if he gains weight on the recommended amount, decrease it by 10 to 20 percent. If he loses weight, increase the amount. It won't take long to find the amount that keeps your Pom "just right"—not too fat and not too thin.

Obesity

Obesity is the most common nutrition-related health problem in dogs. It can increase your Pom's risk of developing liver disease, pancreatitis, and other serious disorders. It can also worsen preexisting conditions such as diabetes mellitus, patellar luxation, and heart disease. Carrying those extra pounds around overworks the heart and makes it harder to breathe. Some overweight dogs can hardly walk, let alone run and play, a situation that only makes the weight problem worse.

Keeping your Pom from becoming obese is lots easier than slimming him down after the fact. Use a portion-controlled or time-controlled feeding plan instead of letting him eat free-choice. (If you use the time-controlled plan, be careful that he doesn't gulp down too much food in the allotted time.) It is also important to limit between-meal treats. Offer your Pom vegetables (raw or cooked) or bits of dry dog food that you've reserved from his daily

ration. The key to keeping slim and fit is to increase your Pom's exercise, even if it's just taking a little longer walk each day. More vigorous exercise is even better, as long as your pal is able to do it—if he has any health problems, ask your veterinarian about a suitable exercise program.

If your Pom is already obese (more than 20 percent heavier than his ideal weight), don't take the "do it yourself" approach—ask your veterinarian about a weight-loss plan, including a complete checkup, diet, and exercise program. Your veterinarian may prescribe a customized diet or one of the therapeutic dog foods especially designed for weight loss. Therapeutic foods work better than nonprescription light foods for major weight loss, but light foods often work well for keeping the pounds off.

Weight Check

Use a hands-on approach to determine if your Pom is the right weight: Run your hands down his sides from front to back. You should be able to easily feel his ribs and "waist"—an indentation between his rib cage and rear legs. If necessary, work your fingers into his coat so you can feel the difference between fat and fur.

Chapter Seven

Training and Activities

Pomeranians are smart cookies, so you probably won't have trouble teaching your pal manners and basic obedience commands. Be forewarned, however: You may have trouble staying ahead of your student. At any rate, you'll both have fun, and training together will make you even better friends.

Why Train My Pom?

When you train your Pom, you'll teach him simple good manners, such as walking on a leash without pulling or not begging at the table, as well as basic obedience commands (*sit, lie down, heel, stay,* and *come*). As a result, he'll be a more pleasant companion. Training will also give your Pom a job, which will ward off boredom and the destructive habits that follow from it. Training can even protect your pal, because you'll have better control of him. For example, if he slipped through the backyard gate and ran toward the street, your command to come would bring him back before he got there. Finally, training reminds your Pom that you're the "pack leader," which makes it easier for you to control him under all circumstances.

Learn to Train

You might not know how to train your Pom right now, but there are several ways to learn:

- **Attend Obedience Classes:** In an obedience class, you'll learn to train your Pom; your Pom will learn basic obedience commands and gain socialization skills from working around other dogs and their owners.
- **Work Individually with a Trainer:** This is a good option if you prefer one-on-one instruction. Private sessions with a trainer are more expensive than classes, but you and your Pom will get more individual attention.

- **Send Your Pom to Obedience School:** With this option, a professional trainer teaches the dog basic obedience commands. Since the trainer works directly with the dog, it's a very effective method of training. Choose a program that includes sessions where you work with your Pom, under the trainer's supervision.
- **Do It Yourself:** This method may work for you, especially if you're an experienced dog owner. If not, you may run into problems that are hard to solve. It helps to have a trainer to consult.

When and Where

You can start training your Pom puppy when he's as young as nine weeks of age. His ability to concentrate will be limited, so keep the lessons short and simple. If you want to enroll your youngster in a "puppy kindergarten" class, get your veterinarian's approval first; his puppy vaccinations may not completely protect him from contagious diseases. Your veterinarian may recommend that you wait until your little friend is at least four months old before exposing him to large numbers of dogs.

On the other end of the age span, there's no limit for training, even if your Pom is a senior. You may have to make a few concessions for an older dog (for instance, he might not be as agile as he once was), but beyond that, you definitely *can* teach an old dog new tricks.

Your training sessions should take place in an area where you and your Pom have some room to move around. If you're just starting out, choose a spot that's free from major distractions such as loose dogs and shouting children. Limit your training periods to one or two per day. Start with about five minutes and gradually work up to fifteen to thirty minutes per session. After each lesson, take a few minutes to play with your student.

Consider your dog's mental attitude before you start a training session. For instance, he won't be in the mood for training if you just got home from work. If he's feeling especially bouncy, take him for a brisk walk or run before you start training. Just be sure to allow some calm-down time before class.

Breed Needs

Training Schedules

If a daily training schedule won't work for you, don't give up: Even a little training time is better than none. You may only be able to work with your Pom for 15 to 20 minutes several times a week. That's okay—you won't reach your training goals quite as fast, but any time spent training your pal will eventually pay off. Plenty of dogs have learned basic manners and obedience commands during lessons that never lasted more than five minutes.

Your Pom's training won't always take place during regularly scheduled sessions anyway; you'll do some training as you teach and reinforce appropriate behavior during the course of your daily routine. In addition, doing a little homework—randomly giving your buddy training tasks throughout the day (for example, making him sit for a treat)—will greatly increase the effectiveness of his more structured lessons.

Equipment

You don't need a lot of equipment to train your Pom, but you do need the right kind of equipment. First, you'll need a training collar—a collar that tightens when pressure is applied on the leash, then loosens immediately when the pressure is released.

Slip-on collars, which are made of chain or nylon, are inexpensive and easy to put on. They don't fit as closely as snap-on collars, so the dog doesn't pick up the handler's signals as quickly. Snap-around collars, which are made of nylon, are harder to put on, but fit closely and provide precise control. They're more expensive than slip-on collars, but still reasonably priced. A snap-around collar is a good choice for your Pom. Pinch collars are made of chain, with blunt prongs that tighten around the dog's neck when pressure is applied. They're wicked-looking, but actually quite safe—unlike the other collars, a pinch collar cannot cut off the dog's air. These collars, which are available in a variety of sizes, are very effective, especially for dogs that pull a lot or otherwise ignore their handlers during training sessions.

The second item of equipment that you'll need is a leash. It should be made of canvas, nylon, or leather, about ½ inch (1.3 cm) wide and 6 feet (1.8 m) long.

Many owners balk at the idea of using a training collar (especially a pinch collar) on their dog, arguing that training collars are cruel, dangerous devices and a regular collar is just as effective. When properly used, a training collar is neither cruel nor dangerous. Constant tension is never applied. Rather, the trainer quickly applies just the amount of correction needed at the precise moment it is needed. When the correction is finished (a matter of seconds), the collar loosens to its original position. Using a regular collar would cause more discomfort, because the corrections would be less effective and necessitate more constant pressure on the collar.

Leash Training

Before you start your training sessions, give your Pom a chance to become familiar with the training collar and leash. Let him wear the collar while he's in the house where you can watch him. Once he's used to the collar, snap the leash on and let him drag it around inside, always keeping him where you can watch him. Praise him when he accepts his training gear.

Next, you'll need to teach your Pom to walk on the leash while you're on the other end. Place the leash on your little pal, and use your voice and a treat to coax him to walk. Don't pull on the leash. When he takes a few

steps, praise him and give him the treat. Continue encouraging him forward as you walk slowly with him at your side, praising him and giving him a treat every few steps.

If your buddy decides to go in a different direction, let him lead for a few steps, then lure him along again. If he won't move, pick him up and carry him a few steps, then put him down and try again. If he bolts ahead on the leash, stop and call him back to you, using a treat if necessary. When he lets the leash go slack, praise him and give him the treat, and then move forward again.

Correction and Praise

There's no way around it: Every dog needs discipline and correction during training sessions. The amount of correction your Pom will need will depend on his personality (stubborn versus tractable) and whether you've let him get away with certain unacceptable behaviors.

Your most effective disciplinary tools will be your voice and the training collar. Reprimands—a simple *"No!"* should suffice—should be spoken firmly and confidently without yelling. A correction with the collar consists of a check—a quick snap on the leash, using only as much force as necessary, followed by an immediate release. It's better to repeat the check than to maintain constant tension on the leash.

Try to be consistent with your commands, your corrections, and your praise. Give commands in a clear, confident voice, always preceding them with your Pom's name (*"Fluffy, sit!"*). Let him know that you expect him to obey, but use correction sparingly. Instead, make it easy for him to do the right thing, then praise him for doing it—or even when he just tries to do it. Whenever possible, choose praise over correction.

If you must correct your Pom, be sure to praise him afterward as soon as possible. Find some little thing that he's done correctly and give him a word of praise and a pat on the head. This will reassure him that your relationship has suffered no permanent damage.

Breed Truths

Timing Counts

Make sure you reinforce the correct behavior by rewarding/praising your pupil when he does what you ask (or even as he's doing it). For example, if you tell your guy to sit, reward him when he does it. If you wait and reward him after you've given him the release command, he'll think you're rewarding him for getting up, not for sitting.

Treats

Everyone works harder when they know they'll be rewarded for their efforts. Your Pom is no different. Because of this, rewarding your buddy when he does what you ask should be the foundation of your training program.

Many trainers recommend using edible treats as training rewards, with good reason: Most dogs love food, especially treat food handed out by their favorite people. It's also a good way to capture your buddy's full attention when you're just starting to train, or when you're teaching something new.

Does this mean you have to use treats to train your Pom? Not necessarily, but if you don't, you need to use a treat substitute, such as ear scratches, head rubs, or a favorite toy. The reward is the important thing, whether it's edible or not. Either way, don't forget to add enthusiastic praise—that's a reward too.

If you decide to use treats to train, choose goodies that are small, so they'll fit easily in your pocket or hand and won't add too many calories to your Pom's diet. Dry (or at least semi-moist) treats will be neater to use. You can use commercially available dog treats (breaking or cutting them into smaller pieces if necessary), dry cat food, or even "people food" such as dry cereal. You may have to try a few different types of treats to find out which one your buddy likes best.

FYI: What is Clicker Training?

Clicker training is a training method that uses operant conditioning, which is based on the concept that animals (and people) associate behaviors and events with either good or bad consequences. The clicker itself can be as simple as the traditional metal child's toy or a more sophisticated device specifically designed for training.

The first step in clicker training is teaching the dog to learn that the "click" sound means he'll get a treat. Since most dogs love treats, this is usually easy to accomplish.

The next steps are a bit more complicated. Let's use the example of teaching your Pom to sit. Once he's learned the first step, wait until he sits on his own, then click and give him a treat (rewarding the behavior). This technique takes patience and time. Some dogs respond well to this method, and will even try different behaviors in an effort to win the treat. Others respond poorly or not at all. If your Pom is one of the latter, you'll need to persuade him to sit, for instance, by using the technique outlined in this chapter. When he sits, click and give him a treat.

After your Pom has figured out that he'll get a click and a treat whenever he sits, it's time to add a cue—a command or signal—for it. When it looks like your pal is going to sit on his own, you give the cue, and then reward his correct response with a click and a treat.

Next, you'll eliminate the click/treat if your Pom sits *without* your cue. Give him a verbal signal such as *"Wrong!"* to let him know that you want him to do something else. This step teaches him that he'll get the treat only if he sits when you tell him to.

Clicker training is very effective, but it requires patience, close observation, split-second timing, and consistency. If you think you'd like to try this training method with your Pom, check with dog schools or trainers in your area to see if they offer classes.

Most of the time, treat training works fine, but there are some situations where it doesn't. You may want to use (or switch to) nonedible rewards if your Pom

- is overweight or has another health problem such as diabetes that requires careful management of food intake;
- gets distracted whenever you move your hand to the pocket where you keep the training treats;
- develops annoying behaviors when you work with him, such as persistently nuzzling your hand looking for treats; or
- isn't interested in working for food (a rare occurrence, but it happens).

Even if you've used treats successfully to train your Pom, you may reach a point where you don't want to pass out a goody for every little thing he does. To wean him off training treats, gradually decrease them, but not in any set pattern, which your clever student will quickly pick up. At the same time, increase the nonedible rewards, regardless of whether you give a treat or not. Continue like this until you're rewarding your pal with treats only every once in awhile—or not at all, if that's your preference.

Basic Pom Manners

In order to be a well-mannered companion, your Pomeranian should know the following commands: *sit, down, come, easy, go lie down, leave it,* and *drop it.*

Sit

To teach your Pom to sit, stand in front of him and hold a treat in front of his nose. Move the treat to a position just above and behind the level of his eyes. When he lowers his rear end and points his nose up, praise him (*"Good!"*) and give him the treat. Next, move the treat farther back so he has to lower his rear end even more to get it. Keep working like this, moving the treat farther and farther back, until he sits. Each time, praise him and give him the treat. Don't forget to use the release command to tell him it's okay to stand up.

Helpful Hints

Okay!

In addition to teaching your Pom basic manners and obedience commands, you should also teach him a release command, a simple word (such as *"Okay"*) to let him know he can relax and move around. For example, if you've put your Pom in a *sit,* the release command tells him he doesn't have to sit anymore.

Once he readily sits for the treat, guide him by using just your hand with no treat. When he sits, praise him and give him a treat from your other hand. Finally, add the spoken command *"Fluffy, sit!"* right before the hand signal. When he sits, praise him and give him a treat.

Most dogs respond well to this method, but if your Pom steadfastly refuses to sit, you'll have to use another training tactic. While he stands beside you, give the command *"Fluffy, sit!"* Use one hand to guide his hindquarters into a sitting position while you keep his head up by holding on to his collar with the other hand. When he sits, praise him and give him a treat. After a few seconds, give him the release command. Keep working with him until he sits without your assistance.

Down

In obedience training, the command *down* means lie down, not get down. To teach this command, have your Pom sit in front of you. Show him a treat and "lead" him with it, moving it away from him and down. When he lowers his front quarters to get the treat, praise him and let him have it. Continue working like this, moving the treat lower and lower, until he lies down. Each time, praise him and give him the treat. Use the release command to let him know when he can get up.

Once he's gotten the hang of lying down for the treat, use just the hand motion to signal him. When he lies down, praise him and give him a treat from the other hand. The last step is adding the spoken command *"Fluffy, down!"* just before the hand signal. When he lies down, praise him and give him a treat.

If your Pom doesn't respond to this training technique, you'll have to show him what you want him to do. Kneel on the floor and have your buddy sit by your left side. Reach over his back with your left hand and gently grasp his left front leg near his body. At the same time, grasp his right front leg near his body with your right hand. Give the command *"Fluffy, down!"* and gently position him by lifting his forequarters slightly off the ground and easing his body down. Once he's lying down, slowly release your hold on his legs and let your left hand rest on his back while repeating the *down* command. Praise him and give him a treat. After a few seconds, give him the release command and let him stand up. Keep working until you no longer have to position him, and then work until he'll lie down while you remain standing.

Come

Anyone who's ever tried to catch a runaway dog can tell you that *come* is one of the most important commands a dog can learn. To teach your Pom to come on command, have him sit, then move away the distance of the leash.

Kneel down and enthusiastically say, *"Fluffy, come!"* Do whatever you need to do to coax him to you: Show him a treat, hold out your arms, pat your knees, or sweet-talk him. Because you're best buddies, he'll probably come bounding up to you. When he gets to you, give him a treat, and then quickly give him the command to sit. You may have to reinforce the *sit* command by guiding him into position. Have him sit for a few seconds, and then praise and reward him. Continue working like this, gradually increasing the distance you move away before calling him. Use a longer leash to practice greater distances, if necessary.

Helpful Hints

Double Up

Ask a friend to help you teach the *come* command. Have your friend hold your Pom and release him when you give the command. Reward your Pom when he comes to you; then hold him and let your friend do the calling.

Easy

A well-mannered dog walks quietly on a leash without pulling. Your Pom doesn't have to *heel*, although that's a useful command too, but he shouldn't be constantly tugging on the leash either. To teach the *easy* command, hold the end of the leash in both hands and anchor them firmly at the level of your waist (hold on to your belt or belt loop if necessary to steady your hands). Give your Pom the command *"Fluffy, let's go!"* and start walking. When Fluffy bounds ahead, as he probably will, say, *"Fluffy, easy!"* and then turn and walk in the opposite direction. If possible, make your turn before he gets to the end of the leash (it might take a few tries to get your timing right). When your little buddy catches up to you, praise him. Repeat the lesson until he'll walk on a slack leash.

Go Lie Down

This command tells your Pom to go to a designated spot and lie down. First, choose the spot—it can be his crate, bed, or even just a special rug. Next, take your pal to the spot and tell him, *"Fluffy, go lie down!"* If you've already taught him the *down* command, he'll probably lie down. When he does, praise him. After five seconds, give him the release command. Gradually increase the distance he has to go to get to his spot. If he doesn't understand what he's supposed to do, gently take him there, give him the command, and praise him when he lies down. Also increase the time he remains in the spot, until he'll stay there for 30 minutes. Always remember to give him the release command when it's okay for him to leave his spot.

Leave It

With your Pom on a leash, walk by a tempting item such as a treat or toy (pre-place the items if you wish). When your pal tries to pick it up, give a quick check on the leash and say, *"Fluffy, leave it!"* Praise him when he obeys.

115

You can reward him with a treat, but cheerful words and ear scratches work well too. Repeat the lesson at home and other locations.

Another method of teaching this command involves holding a treat in your closed fist. When your Pom noses your hand, say, *"Fluffy, leave it!"* and keep your fist closed. When he stops nosing your hand, praise him, then give the release command (*"Okay!"*) and let him have the treat. Continue the lessons until he'll sit quietly without touching a nearby treat until you give the release command.

Drop It!

When your Pom picks up a forbidden object, say, *"Fluffy, drop it!"* and *walk* to him. If he refuses to drop the item, make him obey by physically opening his mouth (roll his upper and lower lips against his teeth and press). When your pal drops the item, praise him and offer him a safe substitute—ideally something that's more appealing than the forbidden item.

If your Pom runs away from you, don't chase him—he'll think you want to play. Instead, ignore him, and then go get something that you know he likes, such as a treat or a toy (the treat will work better). Take the treat or toy to a spot near your Pom and start to eat it (or pretend to eat it, if it's a dog goody) or play with it. Be very enthusiastic about it. Call your Pom to you, and then give him the *drop it* command and trade the treat or toy for the forbidden item. Be sure to praise your friend for obeying. If you gave him a treat, offer him an acceptable toy when he's finished it.

Other Obedience Commands

Once your Pom has mastered the basic training commands, you might want to continue his lessons by teaching him to heel and stay. With these commands you'll have better control over where your pal is, either by your side or not, which is just another step toward making him a well-mannered companion.

Heel

To teach your Pom to heel, position him at your left side and start to walk, giving the command *"Fluffy, heel!"* At the same time, lightly snap the leash to encourage him to walk beside you. Continue to encourage him with your voice and light snaps, if necessary, praising him when he obeys. Your pupil's neck and shoulder should be even with your left leg. If he charges ahead, give the leash a light check and repeat the command to heel. Repeat the check as needed, but never put continuous pressure on the leash. Practice heeling in short, brief sessions. Once your pal heels well while walking in a straight line, add corners, circles, and maneuvers around obstacles.

When heeling, your Pom should sit whenever you stop moving, unless you tell him to do something else. To teach this, have him heel for 15 to 20 seconds, then stop walking and simultaneously tell him to sit. After he sits for a few seconds, give the *heel* command and start walking. After a short distance, stop again and repeat the command to sit. Continue working like this until your pal sits automatically whenever you stop walking.

Stay

During a sitting *stay*, your Pom should remain in a sitting position until you give him the release command. Put his leash on him and have him sit by your side. Give the command *"Fluffy, stay!"* and step a few feet away from him while still holding the leash. Repeat the command. He'll probably try to come with you, especially if you've taught him to heel. If he does, tell him *"No!"* and have him sit again, and then repeat the *stay* command. Have him stay for about 10 seconds, and then give the release command. Continue working on the *stay* until your little pal will remain in place for at least three minutes after just one command. You can also gradually increase the distance you move away. If you like, repeat the lessons using the *down* position instead of the *sit*.

Beyond Basic Training

Once your Pom has mastered the basic obedience lessons on the leash, you might want to try some off-leash work. Before you unsnap that leash, however, make sure your pal obeys all of your commands without hesitation. To work off-leash, have your Pom sit by your side, then simply take the leash off and proceed with a regular training session. If he has lapses in obedience, put the leash back on him and correct as necessary. Concentrate your training on the problem areas, and then remove the leash for another try.

After your Pom has mastered "basic training," you might want to work on advanced obedience training, which involves more complicated exercises such as retrieving objects, jumping hurdles, and extended *stays*.

You can watch dogs performing at this level in obedience classes at many AKC dog shows. If you'd like to do more advanced work with your Pomeranian, consult your local kennel club or professional dog trainer about advanced obedience classes.

Trick-or-Treat

All dogs should know basic obedience commands, but this doesn't mean that everything you teach your Pom has to be serious or even particularly useful for anything beyond sheer entertainment. Tricks can be fun for you to teach and fun for your pal to learn.

You can teach your friend all sorts of tricks. Shaking hands is a classic, but you could also teach him how to play dead, hold the end of his own leash, balance treats or other objects on the end of his nose, roll over, and many others. Think twice before you teach your Pom to "speak" though—you might have trouble getting him to be quiet if he decides to carry on an extended conversation.

Look for books about trick training at the bookstore, on the Internet, or at the public library. You can also check some of the many dog-related websites on the Internet for information about it. If you have a friend whose dog performs tricks, you might ask for help with your trick-training efforts.

Out and About

When you're tired of just hanging around at home, it's time to grab your Pom and head out the door. You and your little friend will find plenty to do out there—in your neighborhood, across town, or across the country.

Walking and Jogging

Walking or jogging will be a lot more fun if you and your Pom do it together. Before you put on your shoes and head for the trail, however, take a little time to consider your friend's comfort and safety.

- Check with your veterinarian to make sure your Pom is in good enough condition for the type and amount of exercise he'll be doing. This is especially important if your pal is a "senior citizen" or has ongoing health problems.
- Keep your Pom on a leash at all times (no exceptions!).
- Make sure your four-footed exercise partner carries proper identification—a collar tag, tattoo, or microchip.
- Avoid areas with loose dogs. Even friendly dogs can be distracting and annoying. Unfriendly dogs can spell disaster for you and your Pom.
- Watch the weather. Don't overdo the exercise when it's extremely hot, especially if it's also humid. Your Pom's thick coat, so nice and cozy on cold winter days, makes it difficult for him to stay cool when the temperature and humidity soar. Rain won't hurt your Pom, but be sure to

dry him off when you get home. If you walk or jog on snow, check your pal's feet frequently and remove any snow that may be balled up between his toes. Be sure to wash off his feet when you get home, to remove any chemicals that may have been used to melt the snow on the sidewalks and streets.

In some towns, dog owners gather informally once or twice a week to walk or jog with their dogs. This is a good way to meet other dog lovers, and it can help your Pom get used to being around other dogs. Ask your dog-owning friends about groups in your town or area. If there aren't any, you might want to organize one yourself.

On the Road

Sooner or later, you'll need (or want) to take your Pom somewhere in the car. Your pal may have an appointment with the veterinarian, or you may just want a change of scenery. Whatever the case, you'll need to get your Pom used to riding in the car before you go.

If possible, start when he's just a puppy, taking him for frequent car rides. Take short ones at first and gradually increase the duration. Don't give up if your little friend is less than enthusiastic about car rides at first. If you do, his only car trips will be the necessary ones, such as visits to the veterinarian, and he really won't want to go. Instead, make your destination somewhere fun, such as the park or a friend's house.

Your Pom will be safer in the car if you follow a few simple rules:

- Keep your Pom in a crate or carrier whenever he's in the car (no exceptions!). You'll both be safer. It's not acceptable to have someone else hold him: He could escape, with disastrous results.
- Place identification and emergency instructions/contact information on your Pom's crate, with duplicates in the glove compartment of your car. If you're incapacitated in an accident, emergency workers will know how to care for your Pom.
- Never leave your Pom in the car on a hot day. Even with the windows rolled down, the temperatures can quickly reach 140°F (60°C) or more, with fatal results.

Before You Go

Traveling with your Pom probably sounds like fun (after all, he's your best friend), but before you load up the car, you'll need to take an honest look at a few things.

First of all, does he enjoy riding in the car? If he doesn't like short trips around town, he's not going to have fun on a five-day road trip. Next, consider your buddy's basic personality. If he's the sociable sort who's always eager to see new sights and meet new people, he'll make an ideal travel companion. If he's a homebody who's more comfortable in familiar surroundings, it's probably better to leave him at home with a dog sitter.

You'll also need to take into account your Pom's health and habits. He should be current on all his vaccinations before you go. If he's a puppy, don't take him on any trips until he's at least 16 weeks old and up-to-date on his vaccinations;

HOME BASICS
I'm Gonna Be Sick!

About 15 percent of all dogs suffer from carsickness, a type of motion sickness that occurs when sensory information about the body's balance and orientation, detected by the vestibular system in the inner ear, doesn't match the visual information from the eyes. In other words, the sensory signals to the brain get crossed up, sometimes with dramatic—and messy—results. The signs of carsickness include anxiety, restlessness, whining, profuse drooling, and vomiting.

Puppies are particularly susceptible to carsickness, possibly because of their immature sensory systems, coupled with anxiety about riding in the car. Anxiety can be a factor for any dog that isn't used to car travel, especially if he's been carsick in the past.

If your Pom is like most dogs, he'll eventually outgrow his carsickness. In the meantime, the following tactics will help make traveling more enjoyable for both of you:

- Get your Pom used to being in his carrier before taking him on his first car trip so he won't be nervous about being confined.
- Reprogram your pal so he associates the car with pleasant activities. At first, just walk him by the car (motor off). When he's gotten used to that, feed him and play with him near the car or in the car, with the motor still off. Finally, repeat the activities while the car idles. Reward him often throughout the entire process.
- Don't feed your Pom a big meal right before a car ride. A light snack or treat might be okay, but don't give him anything more than that. You might try giving him a gingersnap before you go; ginger is a natural antiemetic, which may keep him from vomiting.
- Act happy about riding in the car. Your goal is to convince your buddy that a car ride is fun, not something to dread. If he gets sick, be matter-of-fact about it: Don't get upset and don't punish him. It's okay to comfort him, but don't overdo it.
- Start out with very short trips on smooth roads that don't have a lot of turns and hills. Gradually lengthen your trips, and then add turns and hills.
- If, despite all your efforts, your Pom's carsickness doesn't improve, ask your veterinarian about anti-carsickness medication such as Cerenia (maropitant citrate). Don't give your dog any medication without your veterinarian's approval.

before that age, his vaccinations may not fully protect him. Your pal also needs to be reliably housetrained. If he has any behavior problems, such as persistent barking or furniture-chewing, it's best to get them resolved before you go on any trips.

Guest Work
If you and your Pom will be staying in a hotel, be sure to make reservations ahead of time. Few things can ruin travel more than deciding to stop for the night, only to find that there's no place to stay. Most hotels list their pet

CHECKLIST

Pom Packing

You and your buddy will have more fun when traveling if you take these Pom necessities with you. For convenience, give your buddy his own tote, so you can keep the small items and miscellaneous supplies in one handy place.

- ☐ Carrier or crate (doubles as a bed)
- ☐ Food dish and water dish/bottle
- ☐ Food
- ☐ Treats
- ☐ Bottled water
- ☐ Cooler (optional, but nice for keeping the water cool and storing leftover wet food)
- ☐ Medication, including heartworm preventive and carsickness meds (if needed)
- ☐ Toys
- ☐ Basic grooming equipment
- ☐ Towels
- ☐ Paper towels
- ☐ Baby wipes
- ☐ Plastic bags
- ☐ First-aid kit
- ☐ Health certificate, if you're traveling to another state or country (must be issued within 10 days of traveling; if your trip will last longer than 10 days, you'll need to get another health certificate before coming home)
- ☐ Rabies certificate or tag, unless you have a health certificate (vaccination information is included on the health certificate)
- ☐ Photo of your Pom, in case he gets lost
- ☐ Names and addresses of veterinarians or emergency clinics along the way

policies on their websites, but it's a good idea to confirm that they allow pets when you make your reservation. Whatever you do, don't try to "sneak" your Pom into a hotel that has a no-pet policy.

If the two of you will be staying with a friend or relative, ask beforehand if it's okay to bring your pal. Don't just show up on their doorstep with your fluffy friend (unless you don't want to be invited back).

No matter where you're staying, do your best to be a considerate guest:

- Follow the "rules of the house." If the hotel says your Pom has to be in a crate, keep him in his crate. If your sister doesn't want dogs on her carpet, keep your pal off her carpet.
- Always clean up after your Pom, no matter what he does or where he does it. He's your responsibility, after all.
- If your buddy damages or destroys something, admit it, and then pay for it (that old responsibility thing again).
- If it just isn't working out, take your Pom to a boarding kennel. Don't wait until someone asks you to do it.

Boarding Your Pom

Even though you and your Pom enjoy spending time together, there will be times when you won't be able to take your buddy with you on a trip. When this happens, you'll need to find someone to take care of him. The options available to you will depend on the length of your trip, your resources, and where you live.

You may be able to have a friend or neighbor take care of your Pom while you're gone. If you're going to be gone for only two or three days, you may be able to leave your pal at home, with your friend coming in at least twice a day to take care of him. This arrangement works well for some dogs, but not so well for others. You'll need to isolate your Pom in a dog-proofed area so you don't return to find your house in shambles. For longer trips, it's better to have your friend stay at your house or send your Pom to theirs.

In some towns, you can hire a professional dog sitter to care for your buddy while you're gone. The pros and cons of using a dog sitter are similar to those for a friend performing at-home care, except the dog sitter will probably charge you more.

Boarding your Pom is another option, but carefully check out the boarding kennels in your area before making a decision; you may find a wide disparity in facilities, care, and cleanliness. A reputable kennel will require that your dog be healthy and have up-to-date immunizations. The facility should be clean and well-ventilated, with roomy cages and secure runs for individual exercise sessions. The personnel should be friendly, experienced dog lovers. The boarded dogs should be happy, healthy, and clean.

Unfortunately, the concentration of a large number of dogs in a relatively small area increases the chances of spreading diseases such as kennel cough, even if the kennel has strict standards for health and cleanliness. Kennel

cough, which is aggravating but not usually serious, is probably the most common disease contracted at a kennel; the incidence of more serious ailments, such as distemper, is relatively rare at most reputable facilities. If you decide to board, ask your veterinarian a few weeks ahead of time if your Pom needs vaccinations against kennel cough or other diseases.

You might be able to board your Pom at your veterinarian's hospital or clinic. The care and facilities at most veterinary clinics are usually very good, with the added benefit of readily available veterinary care if your pal needs it. This is a good option for dogs with health conditions (for example, heart disease or epilepsy) that require regular monitoring or medication. Like boarding kennels, some veterinary clinics have a relatively large number of dogs in a fairly small space. However, virtually all veterinary clinics isolate animals with contagious diseases away from those with other problems. Some keep boarded animals and hospitalized ones in separate areas.

Dog Clubs

Dog clubs can be found in many larger towns and cities. In more sparsely populated areas, dog clubs may be made up of members from a wide region of the state, which could mean you'll have to travel farther to get to the

meetings and activities. Some dog clubs accept all breeds, whereas others are devoted to a single breed. In some areas, you may also find clubs that focus on certain activities, such as obedience trials or agility trials.

In addition to holding regular meetings, dog clubs organize activities such as puppy matches—informal dog shows that help inexperienced dogs or owners prepare for the stiffer competition of AKC-recognized shows. Obedience or agility clubs may likewise host activities that serve as practice runs for novice dogs and owners.

For information about dog clubs in your area, check the websites of the American Pomeranian Club (*www.americanpomeranianclub.org*) or the American Kennel Club (*www.akc.org*) or call AKC customer care at (919) 233-9767. A local breeder, pet supply store, or veterinarian may also be able to help you find a club near you.

AKC Events

An intact (not spayed or neutered) Pom registered by the AKC can compete in all AKC-recognized events, including obedience trials, agility trials, and conformation dog shows. Spayed or neutered Poms can't compete in conformation dog shows, which are judged on breeding suitability, but they're eligible for all other events. Any dog can participate in the Canine Good Citizen program.

Canine Good Citizen

The Canine Good Citizen (CGC) program was developed to encourage owners to teach their dogs basic manners. In order to receive the CGC award, the dog must pass a test of the following ten skills:

1. Accepting a friendly stranger.
2. Sitting politely for petting by a stranger.
3. Appearance and grooming (healthy, well-groomed appearance; accepting grooming and examination).
4. Walking on a loose lead, with turns and stops.
5. Walking through a crowd.
6. Sitting and lying down on command; staying in place.
7. Coming when called.
8. Reaction to another dog.
9. Reaction to a distraction, such as a jogger, a chair being dropped, or a rolling crate dolly.
10. Supervised separation (owner leaves dog and goes out of sight).

Local dog clubs or trained individuals (for example, AKC judges, 4-H leaders, or veterinarians) may administer the CGC test. Check with the AKC for a list of clubs and CGC evaluators in your area.

Rally Trials

Rally trials are AKC competitions specifically designed for pet dogs and their owners. They provide a stepping-stone between the Canine Good Citizen program and higher levels of competition, such as obedience or agility trials. Any dog that is at least six months old and registered with the AKC is eligible to compete.

In rally events, the dog and handler move through a course of 10 to 20 "stations," performing specific tasks at or between the stations. While on course, the handler can speak to the dog and use hand signals, but cannot touch the dog. The competition levels include Novice, Advanced, and Excellent, with Novice being the easiest.

At the Novice level, the dog negotiates a course of 10 to 15 stations (with no more than five stationary exercises) while on the leash. In addition to using verbal encouragement and signals, the handler uses physical encouragement (for example, clapping or patting his or her leg) at this level. Novice tasks include changing pace between stations and turning 360 degrees.

ACTIVITIES Agility Trials

Eligible Dogs All AKC-registered dogs six months of age and older; spayed or neutered dogs can participate.

Levels of Competition Novice (beginner), Open (intermediate), and Excellent (advanced). The courses become longer and more complex with each successive level. Dogs or handlers that might have difficulty in regular agility classes can compete at the Preferred level, which has classes with lower jumps and slower completion times.

Classes
- **Standard:** This class contains jumps, weave poles, tunnels, pause tables, and other obstacles, as well as "contact obstacles" (for example, the A-frame, dog walk, and seesaw), which have specially marked zones at each end that the dog must touch with at least one paw.
- **Jumpers with Weaves (JWW):** This class, which has no contact obstacles or pause table, consists of weave poles, jumps, and other obstacles that are negotiated as quickly as possible.
- **Fifteen and Send Time (FAST):** In this class, the dog negotiates 15 obstacles in random order, then completes the "send bonus," two or three other obstacles in a special area where the handler is not allowed.

Scoring Agility classes are scored on both speed and accuracy. Points are deducted for exceeding the standard course time and for errors (for example, displacing a bar on a jump or missing a contact zone).

Titles and Requirements
- **Novice Agility (NA):** Three qualifying scores under at least two judges in Novice Standard classes.
- **Novice Jumper with Weaves (NAJ):** As above, in Novice JWW classes.
- **Open Agility (OA):** As above, in Open Standard classes.
- **Open Jumper with Weaves (OAJ):** As above, in Open JWW classes.
- **Agility Excellent (AX):** As above, in Excellent Standard classes.
- **Excellent Jumper with Weaves (AXJ):** As above, in Excellent JWW classes.
- **Master Agility Excellent (MX):** 10 qualifying scores under two judges in Excellent Standard classes.
- **Master Excellent Jumper with Weaves (MXJ):** 10 qualifying scores under two judges in Excellent JWW classes.
- **Master Agility Champion (MACH):** 750 championship points plus 20 double qualifying scores. The dog earns one championship point for each second under the standard course time in Excellent Standard or Excellent JWW competition. More points are awarded if the dog places first or second in the class. The dog earns one double qualifying score by scoring 100 (clear round) in both the Excellent Standard and the Excellent JWW classes.

At the Advanced level, the dog works off-leash over a course of 12 to 17 stations, with no more than seven stationary exercises. Physical encouragement is still allowed. Advanced tasks include jumping and recall to the front of the owner.

At the Excellent level, the course contains 17 to 20 stations, with no more than seven stationary exercises. The dog competes off-leash, except when performing the honor exercise (the dog maintains a *sit* or *down* at the end of the leash while another dog completes the course). The owner cannot use physical encouragement, but verbal signals and encouragement are permitted. The tasks are more complicated at this level and include exercises such as backing up three steps or a moving stand (standing still while the handler walks around the dog).

ACTIVITIES Obedience Trials

Eligible Dogs All AKC-registered dogs six months of age and older; spayed or neutered dogs can participate. Note: Some obedience trials are limited to a particular breed (specialty trials), but most are open to all breeds (all-breed trials).

Classes
- **Novice:** Basic exercises, including heel on leash and figure eight, heel free, stand for examination, long *sit* (one minute), long *down* (three minutes), and *recall*.
- **Open:** More advanced exercises, including heel free and figure eight, drop on recall, retrieve on flat, retrieve over a vertical obstacle (high jump), broad jump, long *sit* (three minutes), and long *down* (five minutes).
- **Utility:** The most advanced obedience tasks, including signal exercise (responding to hand signals for *stand*, *stay*, *down*, *sit*, and *come*), scent discrimination, directed retrieve, moving stand and examination (dog heels, stands, and stays as handler moves away; stands for examination, then returns to handler), and directed jumping.

Scoring To receive a qualifying score, the dog must earn more than 50 percent of the points for each exercise, with a total score of 170 points out of a possible 200.

Titles and Requirements
- **Companion Dog (CD):** Qualifying scores from three different judges in Novice classes at three AKC-licensed or member obedience trials; a dog must earn the CD title before competing in Open classes.
- **Companion Dog Excellent (CDX):** As above, in Open classes; a dog must earn the CDX title before competing in Utility classes.
- **Utility Dog (UD):** As above, in Utility classes.
- **Utility Dog Excellent (UDX):** A dog with the UD title earns this title by competing successfully in additional Open and Utility classes.
- **Obedience Trial Champion (OTCH):** A dog with the UD and UDX titles earns this title by placing first in three Open and Utility classes and winning 100 points. (The number of points earned depends on the placing and the number of dogs competing in the class.)
- **National Obedience Champion (NOC):** This title is awarded to the dog that wins the AKC National Obedience Invitational, an annual competition of the top obedience dogs in the nation.

A dog that performs the required tasks according to AKC regulations receives a qualifying score (at least 70 out of a possible 100 points). The amount of time it takes the dog to complete the course doesn't affect the qualifying score, but is used to break a tie if two dogs have identical scores.

A dog that earns three qualifying scores from two different judges at one level of competition is awarded the corresponding Rally title—Rally Novice (RN), Rally Advanced (RA), or Rally Excellent (RE). A dog with the RE title can earn the Rally Advanced Excellent (RAE) title by receiving qualifying scores in both the Advanced and the Excellent classes at ten separate trials.

Conformation Dog Shows

In a conformation dog show, each dog is judged according to its official AKC breed standard. Dogs first compete against others of their breed, gender, and age. Class winners continue competing until one individual is selected as Best of Breed—the dog that most closely exemplifies the breed standard. The judge then selects the Best of Opposite Sex. The dogs selected as Best of Breed and Best of Opposite Sex are the top male and female dogs of their breed.

All Best of Breed winners then compete against the other Best of Breed winners of their AKC group. For example, the dog selected as Best of Breed for Pomeranians would compete against all of the Best of Breed winners from the Toy Group. Finally, the group winners compete against each other for the title of Best of Show, the highest honor in a conformation show. When a dog wins a certain number of points at AKC-recognized shows, it earns the title of Champion (Ch.), which is then appended to the beginning of its name (for example, Ch. Oak Hill Scarlet Sunset).

Volunteer Activities

Medical experts, therapists, and educators have finally learned what dog owners have known for years: Dogs are good for people! As a result, dogs are being used in increasing numbers to enhance therapeutic and recreational activities at hospitals, nursing homes, rehabilitation centers, and schools. Usually these dogs are owned by people who volunteer their time and the companionship of their special canine friend.

Volunteer dogs must be well-mannered and reliable, responding calmly to people without jumping up, barking, or biting. They must, of course, be completely housetrained. Some need special skills, depending on where they work; for example, dogs working in medical facilities must not be intimidated or frightened by unusual sights (such as heavily bandaged patients), sounds (such as rattling carts or beeping monitors), smells (such as disinfectant), or activities (such as physical therapy treatments).

Poms have qualities that make them well-suited for certain types of volunteer work. They're small, so they're easy to transport and handle, an important consideration in settings where space is limited, such as hospital rooms. Most Poms are friendly, confident, and outgoing, especially with adults. Some might be a bit wary of children, especially if they don't have a lot of experience with them, but this varies from dog to dog.

Your Pom, in addition to possessing many of the above characteristics, undoubtedly has other special traits. Is he always in a good mood? Does he always seem to know just how you're feeling? Is he calm and well-mannered even when there's a lot going on? If so, there's probably a volunteer job that's just right for him.

Several organizations help owners prepare their dogs (and themselves) for therapy work. Some of these, such as the Delta Society (*www.deltasociety.org*), provide training workshops or home-study training courses, followed by evaluation and registration of dogs that pass the evaluation. Other organizations, such as Therapy Dogs International (*www.tdi-dog.org*), offer only evaluation and registration. The specific requirements for registration vary, but in general the dog must be a minimum age (usually one year), be in good health, and pass a thorough test of manners and obedience. After the dog has been evaluated and registered, the organizations help the owner-dog team find suitable volunteer opportunities.

If you'd like to find out more about volunteer opportunities for you and your Pom, contact hospitals, nursing homes, libraries, and schools in your area. If they don't have a dog volunteer program, they may be able to direct you to a facility that does. Talk to area volunteer agencies. Veterinarians, dog breeders, or groomers might have information about volunteer programs. Keep trying—it might take some time to find just the right opportunity. Once you do, you'll be rewarded by the knowledge that you and your Pom are doing important work helping others in a very special way.

Leash Training

1 Place a leash on your Pom, and without pulling on it, lure him forward with your voice and a treat. Praise him (*"Good!"*) and give him the treat. Continue luring him forward as you walk slowly with him at your side, praising him and giving him a treat every few steps.

2 If he wants to go in a different direction, let him lead for a few steps, and then try to lure him along again.

3 If he refuses to move, pick him up and carry him a few steps, and then put him down and start over.

4 If he pulls ahead on the leash, stop and lure him back to you. When he lets the leash go slack, praise him and give him a treat, and then move forward.

The *Sit* Command

1 Have your Pom stand facing you. Hold a treat in front of his nose, and then move it to a position just above and behind the level of his eyes. When he lowers his rear end and points his nose up, say *"Good!"* and give him the treat.

2 Next, move the treat farther back so he has to lower his rear end even more to get it. Repeat, continuing to move the treat farther back, until he sits. Each time, praise him and give him the treat.

3 Now guide him using just your hand with no treat. When he sits, praise him and give him a treat from your other hand.

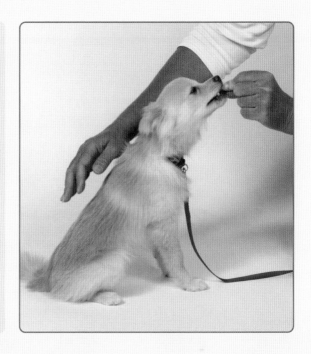

4 Gradually reduce your hand movements until you're using only a small hand signal. Finally, add the spoken signal "*Sit!*" right before the hand signal. Praise him and give him a treat when he sits.

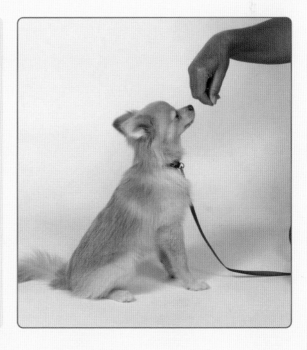

The *Stay* Command

1 Have your Pom sit in front of you. Hold your hand in a "stop" signal in front of his face and say *"Stay!"* Wait for a few seconds, then praise him, give him a treat, and release him by saying *"Okay!"*

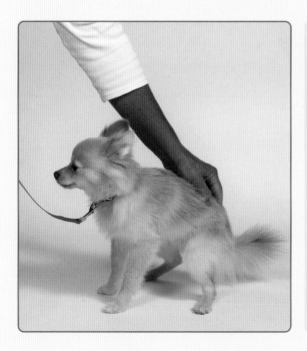

2 If he gets up too soon, put him back in position and try again, but wait less time.

3 Next, have him stay while you move around him. Gradually increase the distance you move away, and then increase the duration of the *stay*. Praise him, give him a treat, and release him each time.

4 Finally, introduce mild distractions and practice in other locations. Keep him on a long line if you're somewhere he could get loose.

Chapter Eight

Grooming

Keeping your Pomeranian well-groomed will take some effort, but all that brushing, combing, and fussing can be fun for both of you. The reward—your best friend strutting his stuff in his fine fur coat—is well worth the time and effort.

Plan Ahead

For some reason, many owners simply assume that their dogs will enjoy being bathed and groomed. Without any warning, they grab their canine companions and unceremoniously plunk them into the bathtub or start attacking them with brushes and combs. It's no wonder that the dog is often less than enthusiastic about grooming.

It doesn't have to be like that. With a little effort, you can make grooming a fun and enjoyable ritual for your Pom. When he's just a puppy, gradually get him used to grooming routines. Brush him frequently, using a soft brush. Keep the brushing sessions short and enthusiastically praise him when he sits still. Wipe his eyes and ears, check his teeth, and handle his paws. If he resists any of these activities, stop and reassure him, then briefly go back to what you were doing. (You don't want him to think that all he has to do is whine and you'll stop.) Praise him when he allows you to continue. Keep working with your youngster until he quietly lets you perform all the necessary grooming chores except bathing (that comes later—when he's at least six months old).

Professional Grooming

If you need some help grooming your Pom—whether on a regular basis or only every once in awhile—a professional groomer can help you out. Just be aware that professional grooming won't relieve you of all your at-home grooming chores, just some of them. Grooming visits usually include bathing, drying, brushing, nail-trimming, and ear-cleaning. A good groomer will also check for signs of skin or ear problems.

SHOPPING LIST

What's in Your Grooming Kit?

✔ **Stiff Bristle Brush:** Use for general brushing. Choose one with wide-spaced, long bristles.

✔ **Wire Pin Brush:** A brush with fine metal "bristles," with or without rubber tips. Use for general brushing.

✔ **Slicker Brush:** A brush with longer wire bristles set in a rubber or foam base. Use to remove dead hair, mats, and tangles.

✔ **Metal Comb:** Use to comb through the coat to check for tangles or mats.

✔ **Mat-Breaking Tool (optional):** Use to break large mats into smaller ones.

✔ **Scissors:** Small ones are more easily handled. Sharp tips make mat-splitting easier, but are more dangerous if your Pom makes an unexpected move.

✔ **Nail Clippers:** Cat nail clippers or human nail clippers work well.

✔ **Shampoo:** Use a canine product; human shampoo can dry your Pom's coat and irritate his skin.

✔ **Conditioner (optional):** Creme rinse or conditioner (canine only) can make your Pom's coat shine and reduce static electricity.

✔ **Sponges (various sizes):** Useful for spot-cleaning and shampooing.

✔ **Ear-Cleaning Solution:** Choose a product specifically for dogs (available at your pet supply store or from your veterinarian).

✔ **Cotton Balls:** Use for spot-cleaning and protecting ears during baths.

✔ **Cotton Swabs:** Use for ear-cleaning (only on easily visible areas).

✔ **Eye Ointment:** Apply to eyes to protect them during a bath.

✔ **Towels:** Use for drying after a bath. A towel placed on the bottom of your sink or tub can keep your Pom from slipping during his bath.

✔ **Hair Dryer (optional):** Speeds up the drying process after a bath. Also useful for spot-drying.

✔ **Soft-Bristled Canine Toothbrush**

✔ **Canine Toothpaste**

Coat Care

You'll need to thoroughly brush your Pom at least two to three times a week (more frequently when he's shedding) to keep his coat and skin healthy. And "thoroughly" means just that: It's important to brush all the way down to the skin, not just the top layer of the coat.

Brush the long part of the coat in sections. Part off a section and brush it with a bristle brush or pin brush. A light misting with water or water plus a bit of conditioner will decrease static electricity, which can cause hair breakage and make the coat difficult to handle. To keep the coat from getting too wet, spritz the air above the section you're working on, so the moisture settles on the hair. When you've finished with this section, part off another one and brush it. Continue until you've brushed the entire coat. Run a metal comb through the coat to check for tangles or mats that you may have missed.

Use just the bristle brush on your Pom's sensitive, shorter-haired areas such as the face, lower legs, and anal area.

If your Pom is shedding or his undercoat is especially dense, use a slicker brush to remove the dead hair. Work gently on small sections so you don't yank out large clumps. Remove the dead hair from the brush as it accumulates.

Mat Attack

Mats—densely clumped wads of hair—
are one of the drawbacks of the Pom's
posh coat. You'll need to use some special tactics to get rid of them:

- Gently tease the mat apart with the
  metal comb.
- Lightly brush the surface of the mat
  with a slicker brush, working your
  way in as the mat loosens up.
- Work a little cornstarch into the mat
  or soak it in hair detangler (human
  or pet). Don't use these remedies at
  the same time or you'll have an
  even bigger mess on your hands.
- Carefully cut through the mat (in
  several places if necessary) with
  scissors or a mat-breaking tool. If
  you use scissors, hold them perpen-
  dicular to the skin surface (or place a metal comb between the scissors
  and the skin) and cut away from the body. Comb to remove the mat.
- Cut out the entire mat with scissors or clippers (cordless ones work
  well for this).
- If your Pom has a lot of mats, have a groomer remove them. This may
  require substantial clipping.

Breed Truths

Double Coat

Your Pom's plush coat is really two
coats in one, known in the dog
world as a double coat. The outer
layer (the topcoat) is long and
straight. Next to his skin he's got a
soft woolly layer (the undercoat)
that tangles easily. To keep his coat
tangle-free and looking its best,
you need to thoroughly brush both
layers.

Bathing

Your Pom will probably need to be bathed only every six to eight weeks, as long as he doesn't come into contact with something that dictates more immediate attention, such as tar, paint, mud, or—every owner's nightmare—a skunk! If you suddenly find yourself with a tarry, painted, muddy, or stinky Pom, you'll need to know how to give him a bath.

On warm days, you could bathe your Pom outside, but you'll probably find it easier to bathe him inside in the kitchen sink or the bathtub. A nonskid rubber mat or towel placed on the bottom of the sink or tub will keep your pal from sliding around.

Brush your Pom thoroughly before his bath. Brush out or remove tangles and mats—they'll only get worse if they get wet. Carefully remove any plant material, such as burrs or sticks, from his coat (don't forget to check his ears and between his toes). If he's gotten into tar or paint, you may need to cut out the affected hair (never use turpentine, kerosene, or gasoline on the coat). If you don't want to cut the coat, soak the affected spots in vegetable or mineral oil for 24 hours and then shampoo.

Helpful Hints

Bath Alternatives

Dry shampoo (available at your pet supply store) is useful for those times when you can't give your Pom a bath or he just needs a little spot cleaning. If you don't have any dry shampoo, you can also use cornstarch: Sprinkle it on the coat, work it in, and then brush it out.

Place small cotton balls in your Pom's ears to keep water and shampoo out of them during the bath. Apply a small amount of eye ointment (available from your veterinarian) to his eyes to protect them.

Adjust the flow and temperature of the water before you put your Pom in the sink or tub. The water should be comfortably warm, not hot. Check the temperature frequently during the bath to make sure it doesn't get too hot or too cold.

Place your Pom in the sink or tub. After he's settled, thoroughly wet his coat. Apply a small amount of shampoo with the sponge (you can always add more if you need to) and lather it up. Massage the lather into your pal's coat. Rinse thoroughly—a handheld sprayer helps, but you can also use a pan or other container. Shampoo and rinse again, if necessary. If you're using conditioner, apply it according to the label directions (diluting the recommended amount in a cup of water makes it easier to work through the coat). Rinse again, making sure you get out any remaining shampoo or conditioner. Squeeze the excess water out of the coat.

Now comes the tricky part—getting that wet dog into a towel before he shakes water all over everything (including you). If he's in the bathtub, you can pull the shower curtain shut and let him shake to his heart's content.

Otherwise, wrap him up in a thick towel and hold him until you can dry him off a bit—and be thankful he's not the size of a St. Bernard!

Next, towel-dry your pooch to get rid of as much excess moisture as possible. Don't get too enthusiastic with the towel or you'll cause tangles. You can finish drying him with a hair dryer (set on warm), but don't put him in a closed-in crate with a hot dryer pointed at him—he could quickly become overheated, with potentially fatal results. On a warm day, you can let him air-dry, but it will take awhile—that woolly Pom coat just doesn't dry very fast. If you keep him inside while he dries, he may get cold even on a hot day, if your air-conditioning is on. If you let him air-dry outside, you'll need to confine him in a clean area such as a patio, so he doesn't find the nearest mud puddle and undo all your good work. You can also put him in a crate, but make sure he has some shade.

Once your Pom is completely dry, brush him again. He probably won't need a full brushing this time—just a touch-up. Run a comb through his coat (to check for tangles), then go over him one last time with the bristle brush if you like. After the final fluff-up, stand back and admire that handsome dog in the luxurious coat!

Stink Bomb

If your Pom has had a close encounter with a skunk, first determine which body parts got blasted (it's usually the face and front end). Next, put on rubber gloves and trim away any long hair in the area. Bathe your odiferous buddy with regular dog shampoo as soon as possible—preferably before the skunk spray dries.

Now you'll need to get rid of the rest of the skunk "perfume." Pet supply stores carry several types of deskunking products—solutions, powders, and shampoos. If you don't have any of these products on hand, you can massage tomato juice or double-strength instant coffee (warm, not hot) into your Pom's coat to cut down the stench. Rinse with water and repeat, if necessary. You can also make your own deskunking compound with ingredients you probably have around the house: Combine 1 quart (.95 L) of hydrogen peroxide (3 percent) with ¼ cup (2 oz.) baking soda and 1 teaspoonful (5 mL) of liquid dishwashing soap in an open container (the mixture will fizz). Mix the ingredients immediately before use. Thoroughly bathe your pal in the mixture, using a cloth to apply it to his face (avoid his eyes and mouth). Throw away any unused mixture.

CAUTION

Skunk Alert!

Skunks can do more than make your Pom smell bad. Skunk spray can irritate his eyes and throat, causing redness, swelling, and pain, especially if he takes a "direct hit" or gets sprayed in close quarters such as a hollow log or burrow. Consult your veterinarian if your Pom shows any of these signs, especially if he's having trouble breathing. Skunks can also carry rabies, so always make sure your buddy's rabies vaccination is up-to-date.

Trimming

Poms don't need a lot of trimming, even if they're show dogs. If your pal is just a pet, you don't have to do it at all. On the other hand, a bit of trimming can keep him neat and tidy:

- **Ears:** Use small scissors to trim the hair on the tips to a rounded shape. To get the right shape, hold the ear with your thumb on the inside, extending slightly beyond the ear tip. Trim the hair using your thumb as a guide.
- **Feet:** Trim around the feet for a neatly rounded look. On the back of the front legs, trim from the foot up to the metacarpal pad—that knobby thing that sticks out on the lower leg. On the rear legs, trim the back of the leg from the foot to the hock.
- **Under the Tail:** Trim the hair around the anus with thinning shears, cutting in the direction of hair growth. Trim excess hair from the base of the tail.

Nail-Trimming

How often your Pom needs his nails trimmed depends on where he spends most of his time. If he's mainly an indoor dog, he may need a trim every three to four weeks. If he goes outside a lot and regularly exercises on hard surfaces, he can go longer in between manicures—about six to eight weeks. If you use a groomer, your Pom will get his nails trimmed during his grooming appointments, but you'll need to check his nails once a week in between visits to make sure they're not getting too long.

It helps to have someone assist you with nail-trimming, especially if you and your Pom are both new to it. Have your assistant hold your dog and talk to him to distract him a bit. Grasp your Pom's paw and gently spread his toes. If his nails are black, just nip the sharp point off the end of each one. If his nails are white, you'll be able to see a pinkish core (the quick) in the center of the nail. Try not to cut into it. Continue trimming until you've done all of the nails. Don't forget the dewclaws if your Pom has them.

If you accidentally clip a nail too short (it happens—even to veterinarians and groomers), your Pom will probably protest loudly and dramatically. Yes, it hurts, but not for long. The nail will also bleed, which may be a bit alarming because bleeding from a nail can be a little harder to stop than bleeding from a similarly sized wound somewhere else on the body. The reasons? There's no soft tissue to compress around the blood vessel (since it's in the middle of the nail) and a dog that's been "quicked" usually bounces around a lot, which increases the bleeding. Don't worry—your Pom won't bleed to death, though he may try to convince you that he will. To stop the bleeding, apply a styptic pencil or anticoagulant stick to the end of the nail or use an old-time home remedy and dip it in a bit of flour. If you don't have these remedies, apply gentle pressure to the end of the nail with a small piece of tissue or cotton for about five minutes. During all the excitement, don't forget to give your "injured" friend lots of sympathy!

Ear Care

Under normal circumstances, your Pom's ears don't need elaborate care, other than an occasional cleaning and periodic checking for foreign bodies (such as burrs or grass awns) or signs of infections or ear mites.

To clean your pal's ears, you'll need cotton balls, cotton swabs, and canine ear-cleaning solution (get it from your veterinarian or at the pet supply store). Never use irritating substances such as alcohol on or in

CAUTION

Now Ear This

Take your Pom to the veterinarian if you notice signs of an ear problem: abnormal odor, discharge, head-shaking, excessive scratching, or pain. If he has a foreign body in his ear, remove it, if possible, but only if you can easily see and grasp it. Otherwise, let your veterinarian take care it.

the ears. Apply a few drops of the ear-cleaning solution to the underside of the ear flap, and then place the tip of the bottle in the ear canal's opening (don't force the tip into the ear canal) and squeeze a small amount of solution into the ear. After letting your Pom shake his head to get rid of the excess solution, massage the base of the ear for 20 to 30 seconds. Use a cotton ball or swab to clean the ear flap. Remove dirt and debris from the ear canal with a cotton ball, not a swab, so you don't push ear gunk farther into the canal.

Dental Care

Proper dental care isn't just a matter of making your Pom look good—it's important for his overall health. Dogs don't usually get cavities, but they're quite susceptible to periodontal disease—gingivitis, periodontitis, and periodontal abscesses. Gingivitis (inflammation of the gums) is most commonly caused by plaque, a soft, colorless scum that coats the teeth. Tartar—a hard yellowish or brown deposit found on the teeth—promotes the formation of plaque. Chronic gingivitis can lead to periodontitis and periodontal abscesses, which can destroy the support structures that hold the teeth in place.

Brushing your Pom's teeth each day with a soft-bristled brush and canine (not human) toothpaste will help prevent plaque formation. Feeding him dry dog food (or one of the newer tartar-control foods) and giving him resilient chew toys may also decrease plaque and tartar buildup.

CHECKLIST

Signs of Tooth Trouble

✔ Difficulty eating
✔ Bad breath
✔ Yellow or brown discoloration of teeth
✔ Loose teeth

✔ Broken teeth
✔ Bleeding gums
✔ Pus between gums and teeth
✔ Retained deciduous teeth (two teeth in one space, in puppies)

Introduce your Pom to home dental care when he's just a puppy. Go slowly, concentrating on making the experience as pleasant as possible. Praise him enthusiastically when he cooperates.

Start by dipping your finger in beef or chicken broth and rubbing it on his teeth. He'll probably think you're a little odd, sticking your finger in his mouth like that, but he'll enjoy the taste of the broth. Next, moisten a gauze pad with broth and rub that on his teeth. Finally, gently brush his teeth with a soft-bristled doggie toothbrush and toothpaste that's formulated for dogs (don't use human toothpaste or baking soda), paying special attention to the gum line at the base of each tooth.

You can use these same tactics to introduce your older Pom to tooth brushing. He may resist your efforts at first, so you'll need to be patient and persistent. Don't give up: By working slowly and praising his good behavior, you'll eventually overcome his resistance.

In addition to home dental care, your Pom also needs to visit the veterinarian at least once a year for a complete dental exam and teeth cleaning, preferably under general anesthesia. Your veterinarian may also apply fluoride or sealants to the teeth, to help strengthen them and reduce plaque accumulation, and take radiographs (X-rays), if needed.

Anal Sacs

The anal sacs (sometimes incorrectly called anal glands) are two small pouchlike structures on either side of the rectum. These sacs, similar to a skunk's scent glands, produce an extremely smelly substance that is normally expressed when the dog has a bowel movement. Dogs often express their anal sacs when they're frightened or excited.

If your Pom's anal sacs don't empty regularly, it will make him uncomfortable. He may scoot his rear end on the ground or chew at his anal area in an effort to relieve his discomfort. Some manuals advise owners to check their dog's anal sacs and express them if there seems to be a problem, but most owners prefer to let their veterinarian handle this rather unpleasant task.

Chapter Nine

The Senior Pomeranian

I t seems like only yesterday that you were bringing your Pomeranian home for the very first time. Now look at him: He's a senior Pom, the very picture of a dignified gentleman—and he's still wearing that great fur coat. Well, maybe he's not all that dignified, but he's still a lot of fun even if he is a little older—and he still looks good in the coat.

Senior Status

Different breeds of dogs have different life expectancies. In general, the smaller the dog, the longer the life expectancy—another advantage of toy breeds. It's quite possible that you and your Pom could enjoy each other's company for 15 years or even longer.

The age at which a dog achieves senior status varies too. Pomeranians are considered seniors when they're about 10 years old, but that's just a breed average. In reality, some Poms have all the traits of a senior when they're eight years old, whereas others don't reach that point until well into their teens.

Breed is just one factor that determines when a dog becomes a senior. Heredity also influences it, just as it does in humans. If your Pom's parents were long-lived, there's a good chance that he will be too. Your pal's health status—both past and present—is also a major factor when it comes to longevity. He's more likely to live longer if he doesn't have any chronic health problems and his weight is normal (not too fat nor too thin). Although this depends somewhat on heredity too—healthy dogs have healthy parents—it also depends on the health care you've given him up to this point.

Senior Traits

No two Poms are exactly alike, regardless of whether they're seniors or not. Nevertheless, some traits occur more frequently with advancing age. You may notice the following in your senior pal:

- **Variable Independence:** The stereotypical senior dog is independent and set in his ways. This may describe your Pom, or he may seem to get more dependent on you as he ages.
- **Grumpiness:** Your Pom may become increasingly cantankerous with advancing age. This may be a sign of cognitive problems, or he could have a health condition that's causing chronic pain.
- **Forgetfulness, Confusion, and Lapses in Attention:** These are other signs of a cognitive deficit, but other health problems can cause them too.
- **Less Energy:** Your senior buddy may spend more time napping and less time exercising than he did when he was younger, but this isn't always the case. Some dogs stay active well into their senior years.
- **Less Playfulness:** This also varies depending on the dog's personality. Your Pom may maintain his playful spirit throughout his life.
- **Health Problems:** Your senior Pom may have chronic health problems such as arthritis, heart disease, or kidney problems that limit his activity and affect his quality of life. This doesn't mean he has to spend all of his time lying around.
- **Housetraining Mistakes:** If your senior Pom has more "accidents," there's probably a good reason. He may have a cognitive problem that's caused him to forget his training, or he may have another health problem that makes it harder to get outside when he needs to go.

Keeping Your Senior Healthy

Keeping your senior Pom healthy is an essential part of helping him enjoy his later years. If your pal is healthy, he'll have a better quality of life, which of course will improve your quality of life too.

Proper Nutrition

Your senior Pom's nutritional needs vary, depending on his age-related physiological changes and overall health.

Maintaining proper body condition—neither too fat nor too thin—is especially important for older dogs. Weight gain is a problem for many senior dogs because they become less active at the same time their metabolic rate is slowing down. If your senior Pom is one of these "couch potatoes," you'll need to take action before he becomes seriously overweight. Start by switching him to a completely balanced senior food. These products contain less fat and fewer calories than regular adult maintenance foods, but have more fiber, so your buddy will feel satisfied even though he's consuming fewer calories. Adding a 20-minute walk or other light exercise to your Pom's daily routine will also help keep him slim and trim. It may work so well that that you won't have to implement any dietary changes at all.

Some dogs baffle their owners and veterinarians by losing weight as they age. Sometimes this occurs when the senior dog eats less because of chronic health issues—

Breed Needs

Nutrition Musts

Feed your senior Pom for optimal health:

- Feed a completely balanced food (check the label).
- Limit table food to 10 percent of his daily calories.
- Don't feed too many snacks, especially if your pal is overweight.
- Always provide plenty of fresh clean water.

dental problems, cancer, heart disease, and many others. Some older dogs stop eating because their senses of smell and taste become less acute; a dog seldom eats what he can't smell or taste. Other dogs eat normal amounts, or even increased amounts, but lose weight because digestive problems keep them from properly digesting food or absorbing nutrients.

If your senior Pom is underweight, take him to your veterinarian to find out if the cause is an underlying health problem. If this is the case, your veterinarian can then advise you about treatment, which may include dietary recommendations, such as a prescription food.

If your Pom's weight problem is caused by less defined age-related changes, your veterinarian may recommend changing your pal's food to one that contains greater amounts of high-quality fat, which increases both the taste and the calorie count. A change in feeding schedule may also help. For example, your senior Pom might digest his food more easily if you feed him three or more smaller meals a day rather than just two.

Changes in body condition aren't the only nutritional challenges that older dogs face. Protein metabolism decreases with age, so your senior Pom needs up to 50 percent more protein than he did when he was younger, even if he appears to be the picture of health. Protein deficiency can lead to weakness, muscle wasting, and immune system impairment, which can increase your friend's susceptibility to illness. To ensure adequate protein intake, the protein content of most senior foods is similar to that of puppy foods.

Exercise

When your Pom was younger, you probably didn't have to do much to make sure he got enough exercise. In fact, he probably did it all on his own. Getting him up and moving may be more difficult now that he's older, but it's more important than ever. Exercise provides the following benefits:

- Improves cardiovascular fitness.
- Prevents weight gain.
- Prevents muscle wasting.
- Increases mobility and joint range of motion.
- Provides mental stimulation.

Your pal is more likely to enjoy exercising if the two of you do it together, but you'll probably need to make a few adjustments in your exercise routine. First, get your veterinarian's approval before you start any kind of exercise program. Next, you'll need to tailor the program to your Pom's capabilities. For example, if he has arthritis or another problem that affects his mobility, he probably won't enjoy jogging or a vigorous game of Frisbee, but walking may suit him just fine. Timing matters too; he may do better with several short walks throughout the day rather than one long one. If you've been a little lax on the exercise program, start slowly and gradually increase his exercise as he gets back in shape. For example, start with a five-minute walk at a relatively slow pace and work up to twenty to thirty minutes at a faster pace. If the exercise makes your Pom stiff and sore, cut back on the intensity. If that doesn't help, ask your veterinarian about pain-relieving medication, which will make your buddy more comfortable during and after exercise.

Dental Care

Proper dental care is especially important for senior dogs because dental problems can lead to eating problems and subsequent weight loss, which can ultimately compromise overall health. Senior dogs with compromised immune systems may be particularly susceptible to diseases after weight loss.

To keep your Pom's teeth and mouth in optimal condition:

- Brush his teeth every day with a soft-bristled brush and toothpaste formulated for dogs.

- Feed him dry food or a tartar-control food, unless your veterinarian recommends another diet.
- Give him resilient toys and artificial bones to chew on. Don't give him real bones, which can splinter and damage his teeth and injure his mouth, as well as the rest of his digestive tract.
- Take him to the veterinarian at least once a year for a complete oral examination (including X-rays if needed) and teeth cleaning.

Health Exams

Yearly health exams are fine for younger dogs, but your senior Pom needs them every six months. Since his body systems don't work quite as well as they did when he was younger, he's more vulnerable to health problems. If he develops one, it may be more difficult for him to respond to treatment. For these reasons, it's important to catch health problems as soon as possible.

At your Pom's health exam, you can also ask your veterinarian any questions you have about taking care of your senior Pom.

In addition to a complete physical examination, your veterinarian may recommend certain laboratory tests. These might include the following:

- **Complete Blood Count (CBC):** This test determines the numbers and types of cells in a blood sample, which can indicate the presence of problems such as anemia, infections, and leukemia, as well as indicate a response to treatment, if needed.
- **Blood Chemistry Panel:** This test measures electrolytes, enzymes, and chemical elements such as calcium, potassium, and

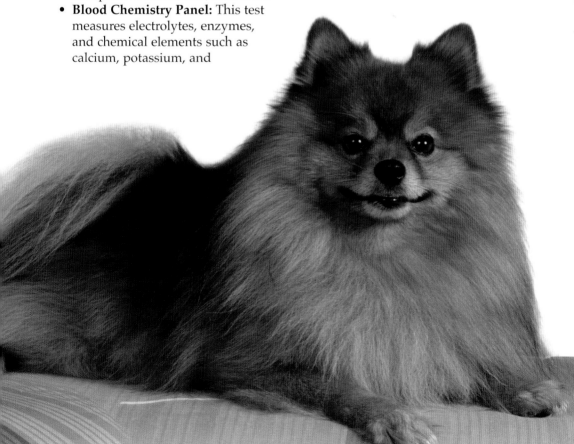

sodium. These measurements can help your veterinarian evaluate organ function (especially kidneys and liver), prescribe therapy, and monitor treatment response.

- **Urinalysis:** This test evaluates kidney function and also provides information about substances in the urine (for example, blood, protein, white blood cells, or glucose) that may indicate certain diseases.
- **Fecal Examination:** Microscopic examination of a stool sample can indicate whether your Pom has intestinal parasites (worms), which can cause digestive problems and anemia.

Senior Health Problems

Dogs, like people, often develop health problems as they get older. Recognizing the symptoms and understanding the treatment options can help you take better care of your buddy should the need arise.

Arthritis

Many senior dogs are plagued by arthritis (osteoarthritis or degenerative joint disease), a painful and progressively destructive joint inflammation. Arthritis occurs when other conditions (abnormal conformation, injuries, developmental disorders, congenital problems such as patellar luxation, and age-related "wear and tear") put abnormal stress on the joint. It starts with damage to the joint cartilage, which impairs its function, causing a self-perpetuating cycle of progressive cartilage damage, more functional impairment, and pain.

If your Pom has arthritis, he may be sore and stiff after he's been lying around, with some improvement once he's been up and moving for a while. You may notice that some tasks are more difficult for him than they used to

BE PREPARED! Senior Vaccinations

Just because your Pom has reached seniorhood doesn't mean he's through with vaccinations. It's true that the core vaccinations (distemper, infectious hepatitis, parvovirus, and rabies) last a lot longer than once thought—up to seven years for some of them—but it's never a good idea to gamble with your pal's health.

Ask your veterinarian what vaccinations your old friend needs. If he or she recommends annual vaccinations, don't be afraid to ask why—the veterinarian should be able to explain the reasons for it. If you're not satisfied with the explanation, get a second opinion from another veterinarian. You can also ask your veterinarian to do a laboratory test to check your Pom's levels of antibodies to specific diseases. If the antibody level is too low to offer protection, your friend needs the vaccination. If they're sufficiently high, he doesn't.

FYI: Health Warning Signs

Warning Sign	Possible Cause
Limping, lameness	Arthritis
Change in appetite or weight (increase or decrease)	Liver, kidney, or heart disease; oral problems (dental problems, mouth tumors); endocrine problems (diabetes, Cushing's disease, hypothyroidism); abdominal tumors; internal parasites.
Chewing abnormality (difficulty chewing, dropping food, chewing on one side, bad breath)	Dental problems; mouth tumor; sinus infection. Note: Loss of appetite, weight loss, sneezing, or nasal discharge sometimes occur with these problems.
Exercise intolerance	Heart disease; endocrine problems (hypothyroidism, Cushing's disease, diabetes); anemia.
Increased water consumption (usually accompanied by increased urination)	Kidney or liver disease; endocrine problems (diabetes, Cushing's disease).
Changes in urination (increased frequency, straining, passing blood, inappropriate urination, dribbling)	Urinary tract problems, including kidney disease, infections, urolithiasis (urinary "stones"), and tumors; prostate disease; endocrine problems (diabetes, Cushing's disease).
Behavioral changes (circling, forgetfulness, aimless wandering, seizures)	Cognitive dysfunction ("canine Alzheimer's"), brain tumors, kidney disease.

be, such as climbing stairs or playing ball. If he exercises strenuously, he may be very sore the next day.

Arthritis can't be cured, but it can be treated and managed. The most effective treatments usually combine several types of therapy, including medication. (Always check with your veterinarian before giving your dog any medication or supplement.) Below are some ways you can help to minimize your Pom's discomfort from arthritis pain.

Weight Control Extra weight means extra stress on your Pom's joints. If your buddy is overweight, your veterinarian can recommend a suitable weight loss program.

Exercise Mild exercise such as walking increases muscle mass (which supports affected joints), promotes joint flexibility, and makes weight control a little easier.

Massage and Physical Therapy Gently massaging and manipulating your Pom's sore joints and the surrounding muscles can make him more comfortable and enhance joint flexibility.

Joint-Supportive Agents Oral "nutraceuticals" (nutrients that have medicinal properties) such as glucosamine and chondroitin sulfate may promote cartilage repair. Other supplements that might help include omega-3 fatty acids (fish oil), vitamin C, methyl sulfonyl methane (MSM), and green-lipped mussel powder. Nutraceuticals don't always work and if they do, it may be weeks or months before you see an effect. Your veterinarian can also inject your Pom with polysulfated glycosaminoglycan (Adequan), a joint-supportive agent that helps prevent cartilage damage and may promote healing.

Non-Steroidal Anti-Inflammatory Drugs (NSAIDs) Carprofen (Rimadyl), etodolac (Etogesic), and other NSAIDs work more quickly and reliably than nutraceuticals but can cause serious side effects such as gastrointestinal bleeding, liver problems, and kidney failure. Some NSAIDs also cause further joint damage by altering cartilage cell function. In addition, NSAIDs can indirectly contribute to joint damage if they provide so much relief that it leads to overexertion and injury.

Corticosteroids Prednisone and other corticosteroids decrease inflammation and relieve pain, but also cause undesirable side effects such as hair loss, impaired wound healing, and immune suppression, especially with extended use.

Environmental Changes A few modifications around your house and yard will make life easier (and safer) for your Pom. For example, keep him in hazard-free areas that have nonskid footing. Remove obstacles and build ramps to make it easier for him to get around. Physically assist him, if necessary. Place soft bedding in easily accessible areas.

Cognitive Dysfunction Syndrome

Cognitive dysfunction syndrome (CDS) is a brain disease of senior dogs that is somewhat similar to Alzheimer's disease in people. It affects the dog's cognitive ability (thinking ability), which in turn leads to various types of behavioral abnormalities. Cognitive dysfunction syndrome is not part of the normal aging process, but a study by the University of California–Berkeley found that nearly two-thirds of dogs between the ages of 11 and 16 had at least one sign of CDS. The percentage of dogs affected increases as the dogs get older.

The following are some of the symptoms of CDS:

• Withdrawing from interaction with family members.
• Not recognizing family members or other familiar people.
• Staring at walls or into space.
• Pacing or wandering aimlessly.
• Unusual sleeping habits (sleeping more during the day or less at night).
• Getting lost in familiar places such as the home or yard.
• Getting trapped in corners or behind furniture.
• Difficulty learning new things (tasks, commands, or routes).
• House soiling.
• Not responding to name.

If you think your senior Pom may have CDS, you need to take him to your veterinarian for a complete workup, which will include a detailed history, behavioral analysis, physical examination, blood tests, and urinalysis. Since there are no definitive tests for CDS, it's often diagnosed by ruling out other problems that have similar symptoms.

Unfortunately, CDS can't be cured, but treatment with a medication called Anipryl (l-deprenyl) can alleviate some of the symptoms. Other measures you can implement to improve your Pom's quality of life include proper nutrition, exercise, mental stimulation with games and activities, and of course, your companionship.

Vision Loss

Vision loss commonly occurs in dogs as they age. It doesn't happen overnight, but rather occurs over years. The slow onset plus the dog's remarkable ability to cope with diminishing sight fools many owners into thinking their dogs can see just fine.

If your senior Pom has some vision loss, you may be upset about it, but he doesn't need your sympathy. He needs you to help him adjust to his diminishing vision, so he can get on with his life. You can do this by concentrating on his abilities, not his limitations. A few simple steps will keep your Pom safe and help him adjust to his vision loss. Keep your furniture where it's always been, so he can navigate easily through the house. If he spends time outside, leave your lawn furniture in one place out there too. Use barriers or fences to keep him away from hazardous structures such as stairs, balconies, hot tubs, and swimming pools. Make it easy for him to find his food and water by always placing his dishes in the same location, which of course should be easily accessible for him.

Your Pom may have vision loss, but most of his other senses probably still work, so make the most of them. Talk to him. Pet him (remember to speak first so you don't startle him). Use a clicker, bell, or your voice to help him find you in the house or yard. Give him dog-safe toys that are highly scented or equipped with squeakers or bells.

Vision loss doesn't mean you and your pal can't get out and about. Of course, you'll need to keep him on a leash whenever he's outside your house or yard, just as you would if he could see perfectly. When you introduce strangers to your Pom, instruct them to speak to him without touching him and then let him approach them when he's comfortable.

Hearing Loss

Hearing loss is also common in older dogs, just as it is in older people. Like vision loss, hearing loss occurs gradually.

If your Pom has a hearing deficit, you may notice that he doesn't react to sounds that once got his attention. He may sleep more soundly. Instead of barking when the doorbell rings, he may not even look up. And, most disconcerting, he may not respond to you when you say his name.

You can check your Pom's hearing by conducting an easy test with a metal saucepan and a spoon. Stand where he can't see you and tap vigorously on the pan with the spoon. The sound produced falls in a range that's usually audible to dogs even with moderate hearing loss, so if your pal doesn't respond, it indicates that his loss is fairly severe. If he responds but repeatedly looks around as if he's trying to locate the sound, it could mean that the loss is greater in one ear.

Unfortunately, there's no treatment for hearing loss in dogs, although some research is being done to develop a canine hearing aid. Most dogs seem unperturbed by their deficit and simply learn to rely on their other senses.

You can help your Pom compensate for his hearing loss by using the following tactics:

- Speak loudly and clearly in low-pitched tones.
- Use hand signals to communicate. You can also teach him to respond to a flashing light (for example, turning your porch light off and on to call him to the house). If he also has some vision loss, use touch instead of hand signals.
- If you want to get his attention from across the room, toss a soft toy near him.
- Enter his field of vision before you touch him. If he also has a vision deficit, stomp on the floor or tap with a cane so he can feel the vibrations as you approach.
- Make sure other people are aware of your Pom's hearing loss. Instruct them to make sure he can see them or feel their vibrations before they touch him.

Heart Disease

Heart disease is a common affliction of older dogs, with mitral insufficiency accounting for most of the cases. In this disease, the mitral valve—the valve between the left atrium and left ventricle—becomes thickened and doesn't close properly, which allows some of the blood to leak back into the left ventricle. As a result, the heart must work harder to pump the blood. The condition worsens over the years until finally the heart begins to fail.

If your senior Pom has mitral insufficiency, you may find that he can't exercise as much as he once did. He may seem short of breath, even at rest, and his tongue may be a bit bluish instead of a normal healthy pink. He may have a persistent cough, especially at night. If you notice any of these symptoms, it's important to take your pal to your veterinarian as soon as possible. He or she will examine your buddy and do a thorough workup, which will likely include blood tests, an electrocardiogram (ECG), and an echocardiogram.

Treatment for mitral insufficiency consists primarily of various types of medication to help the heart work more efficiently and to relieve fluid accumulation in the lungs. Some veterinarians recommend low-sodium prescription food, which also helps lessen fluid retention. Mitral insufficiency can't be cured, but with appropriate treatment a dog with this disease can have many years of high-quality life.

Kidney Failure

The kidneys have several important functions, namely, removing metabolic waste products from the blood, regulating the volume and composition of body fluids, producing hormones that stimulate red blood cell production, and controlling blood pressure. Chronic kidney failure occurs when the kidneys can no longer perform these functions, which are vital to your Pom's health. Aging is the most common cause.

With chronic kidney failure, kidney function decreases slowly over a long period of time, resulting in the gradual appearance of symptoms: increased water consumption, increased urination, listlessness, vomiting, bad breath, loss of appetite, weakness, and weight loss. If your pal has any of these symptoms, contact your veterinarian immediately. In addition to performing a physical examination, he or she will also do blood tests and a urinalysis to evaluate kidney function and rule out other possible causes of the symptoms.

Kidney failure can be life-threatening. If your Pom has it, he'll need to be hospitalized for treatment, which will include intravenous fluids, medication, diet therapy, and supportive care. When he's recovered enough to leave the hospital, you'll need to continue some of his treatments at home. Your veterinarian will also want to recheck him frequently to monitor his progress.

Even though kidney failure is a serious disease, you can help your Pom have a better quality of life (and possibly a longer one) by working with your veterinarian and providing diligent home care.

CAUTION

Cancer

Cancer affects dogs of all ages, but it's especially prevalent in seniors. In fact, the disease is responsible for nearly half of all deaths in dogs over the age of 10. Cancer can affect virtually any system in the body, starting in one place and spreading, via metastasis, to remote locations. Its symptoms range from obvious lumps or sores to obscure abnormalities that can be detected only with special diagnostic techniques.

A diagnosis of cancer isn't an automatic death sentence. Dogs with the disease are often treated with the same types of therapy that are used to treat people, including surgery, chemotherapy, and radiation therapy. Treatment doesn't always cure the cancer, but it can produce a remission that significantly extends the dog's life.

Saying Good-bye

It's always difficult to say good-bye to the special friend with whom you've shared so much. It's even harder when you're the one who must make the decision to end your friend's life. Nevertheless, there are certain situations in which euthanasia must be considered, especially with senior dogs. Even with the best of veterinary care, there are diseases and conditions, such as advanced cancer or cognitive dysfunction syndrome that cannot be cured. Sometimes

dogs with these conditions can live fairly normal lives for variable periods of time, but in other cases prolonging life means prolonging pain and suffering.

There's no simple way to make the decision about euthanasia. If you're faced with the responsibility of making this decision, ask yourself and your veterinarian the following questions about your Pom:

- How well can he eat, drink, get around, and control his bodily functions, such as elimination?
- Is his condition getting worse, despite treatment?
- What is the outlook for recovery or significant improvement?
- Is he in pain and if so, can it be adequately controlled with medication and/or lifestyle changes?
- Is he fighting to live or just waiting to die?

Try to answer the questions as honestly as possible, even if the answers upset you. Although your feelings are important, don't decide against euthanasia simply because of the grief you will experience. Keep in mind how sad you would be if your friend had to suffer needlessly.

Euthanasia is performed by administering an injection of a drug that is similar to an anesthetic, only much stronger. The dog first loses consciousness and then passes on quickly and painlessly. Some owners prefer to remain with their dogs during euthanasia, but it can be very upsetting, even if you know you made the right decision. For this reason, you may choose to share some quiet time with your Pom and then leave the room. Either choice is fine; do whatever you feel is most comforting for you and your special friend.

Resources

Organizations

American Kennel Club
Customer Service
5580 Centerview Drive
Raleigh, NC 27606
Phone: (919) 233-9767
www.akc.org

American Pomeranian Club
Jane Lehtinen, President
1517 8th Street
Virginia, MN 55792
www.americanpomeranianclub.org
Note: Check the website for the
most current information.

Canadian Kennel Club
200 Ronson Drive, Suite 400
Etobicoke, ON, Canada M9W 529
Phone: (416) 675-5511
www.ckc.ca

United Kennel Club
100 E. Kilgore Road
Kalamazoo, MI 49001-5598
Phone: (269) 343-9020
www.ukcdogs.com

Magazines

AKC Gazette
AKC Family Dog
Contact AKC for subscription
information.
www.akc.org

Dog Fancy
Dog World
P.O. Box 6050
Mission Viejo, CA 92690-6050
Phone: (949) 855-8822
www.dogchannel.com

The Pom Reader
8848 Beverly Hills
Lakeland, FL 33809-1604
Phone: (863) 858-3839
www.dmcg.com

The Pomeranian Review
Brenda Segelken, Editor
11139 E. Camelot Avenue
Effingham, IL 62401
Phone: (217) 347-5731
www.americanpomeranianclub.org

Health Organizations

American Veterinary Medical
   Association
1931 N. Meacham Road, Suite 100
Schaumburg, IL 60173-4360
Phone: (800) 248-2862
www.avma.org

American Animal Hospital
   Association
12575 W. Bayaud Avenue
Lakewood, CO 80228
Phone: (303) 986-2800
www.healthypet.com

AKC Canine Health Foundation
P.O. Box 900061
Raleigh, NC 27675-9061
Phone: (888) 682-9696
www.akcchf.org

Morris Animal Foundation
10200 E. Girard Avenue, B430
Denver, CO 80231
Phone: (800) 243-2345
www.morrisanimalfoundation.org

Index

167

THE TEAM BEHIND THE *TRAIN YOUR DOG* DVD

Host **Nicole Wilde** is a certified Pet Dog Trainer and internationally recognized author and lecturer. Her books include *So You Want to be a Dog Trainer* and *Help for Your Fearful Dog* (Phantom Publishing). In addition to working with dogs, Nicole has been working with wolves and wolf hybrids for over fifteen years and is considered an expert in the field.

Host **Laura Bourhenne** is a Professional Member of the Association of Pet Dog Trainers, and holds a degree in Exotic Animal Training. She has trained many species of animals including several species of primates, birds of prey, and many more. Laura is striving to enrich the lives of pets by training and educating the people they live with.

Director **Leo Zahn** is an award winning director/cinematographer/editor of television commercials, movies, and documentaries. He has directed and edited more than a dozen instructional DVDs through the Picture Company, a subsidiary of Picture Palace, Inc., based in Los Angeles.

The enclosed training DVD is provided as bonus material for the consumer. It is published independently, and therefore does not necessarily reflect the opinions, views, or practices of the author and/or Barron's Educational Series, Inc. Neither the author nor Barron's shall be held responsible for any injury, loss, expense, or damage suffered or incurred by any person or animal who participates in the training exercises demonstrated in the enclosed video presentation.